Test Your Grammar and Usage for FCE

Peter Watcyn-Jones
and Jake Allsop

PENGUIN ENGLISH

Pearson Education Limited

Edinburgh Gate

Harlow

Essex CM20 2JE, England

and Associated Companies throughout the world.

ISBN-13: 978-0-582-45174-2

ISBN-10: 0-582-45174-4

First published 1996

This edition published 2002

Sixth impression 2006

Text copyright © Peter Watcyn-Jones 1996, 2002

Text copyright © Jake Allsop 2002

Designed and typeset by Pantek Arts Ltd, Maidstone, Kent

Test Your format devised by Peter Watcyn-Jones

Illustrations by Phil Healey and Ross Thomson

Printed in China   SWTC/06

Published by Pearson Education Limited in association with Penguin Books Ltd, both companies being subsidiaries of Pearson plc.

For a complete list of the titles available from Penguin English please visit our website at www.penguinenglish.com, or write to your local Pearson Education office or to: Marketing Department, Penguin Longman Publishing, Edinburgh Gate, Harlow, Essex CM20 2JE

Contents

To the student

If you are going to take the Cambridge First Certificate exam, you will find the tests in this book very helpful. They will help you practise a lot of the structures and language that you will need in the Use of English paper. Many of them also have useful information on what examiners are looking for.

There are two parts to the book:

The first part (sections 1–4) gives practice in the most important areas of language relevant to the exam as a whole. Sections 1–3 cover verb constructions such as phrasal verbs and verb + noun combinations; use of prepositions; and sentence construction. Section 4 deals with common problems, such as the use of *make* and *do*, *some* and *any*, and when to use the infinitive (*do*, *to do*) or the *-ing* form (*doing*).

The second part (sections 5–9) deals with particular tasks in the Use of English paper, namely:

- cloze texts with multiple choice to test knowledge of vocabulary
- cloze texts without multiple choice to test structural words and collocations (words that go together, such as *make a promise*, *tell a lie*, *go to bed*)
- sentence transformation
- error correction
- word building.

There are also two tests (59 and 60) which deal specifically with grammatical terminology, including the names of tenses.

There is a key at the back of the book so that you can check your answers.

You don't need to work through every test in this book. Instead, you can concentrate on those areas where you feel you need more practice.

Don't forget to keep a record of new items that you come across, and try to use these items as much as possible before the exam. In particular, we suggest that you don't just note down a new word or expression, but that you also write and learn a phrase containing it. For example, don't just write *on purpose*: put it in a sentence like *I'm sorry I broke your glasses, but it was an accident: I didn't do it **on purpose***.

If you want to improve your vocabulary for FCE as well as your grammar, you might like to use the Penguin book which accompanies this one. It's called *Test Your Vocabulary for FCE*. There are several other titles in the *Test Your* series which you will also find useful, including *Test Your Phrasal Verbs* and *Test Your Prepositions*.

Good luck in the exam!

Peter Watcyn-Jones   Jake Allsop

Verbs

When you are revising verbs, the things to concentrate on are:

● Form

Think about which verbs take -s and which take -es, e.g. *read-reads*; *watch-watches*. Learn the irregular verbs: you can categorize them according to how they change, e.g., AAA (no change), as in *put-put-put*; ABC (three different forms), as in *speak-spoke-spoken*; ABA, as in *come-came-come*.

● Tenses

Remember that the tense of a verb is not just about time, i.e., I *did it* **yesterday**, *I will do it* **tomorrow**; but also about our attitude to the event. For example, there is a difference between *What did you do today*? and *What have you done today*? The simple past asks about what a person did e.g. at work today, assuming that work is finished for today; the present perfect is asking what the person has done so far today and what effect that has on the present. Think, too, of the difference between *He'll do it* and *He's going to do it*; or *What do you do*? and *What are you doing*?

● Verb phrases

Verbs are often in collocations, i.e., set expressions with other words, for example:
with nouns: *to take place, to make fun of*
with adjectives: *to turn red, to go sour, to run dry*

The most common and most useful are probably phrasal verbs, for example:
with adverb   *to stand up, to go away*
with preposition   *to look for* (something), *to bump into* (someone)

'What have you done today?'

1 Fill in the verbs

Put the verbs in brackets in the passage below into the correct tenses. There is an example at the beginning (0).

THE CAR THIEF

My cousin and her husband live in Hanwell, one of the suburbs of London. One morning they (0) ___woke up___ (wake up) to find to their dismay that their car (1) _____ (steal) from outside their house. They immediately (2) _____ (phone) the police to report the theft, before (3) _____ (leave) for work by bus.

When they (4) _____ (return) home later the same day, they (5) _____ (find) to their surprise that their car (6) _____ (bring back) and was parked in its usual place outside their house. Under one of the windscreen wipers (7) _____ (be) a small envelope.

They quickly (8) _____ (open) it and (9) _____ (find) a note (10) _____ (apologize) profusely for 'borrowing' their car. The man who (11) _____ (write) it explained that he (12) _____ (not have) a car himself, and his wife (13) _____ (go) into labour in the middle of the night with their first baby. So he (14) _____ (hope) they (15) _____ (not mind) too much that he (16) _____ (take) their car without their permission in order to run her to the hospital, as it was something of an emergency.

By way of compensation, he (17) _____ (enclose) two tickets for the West End show *Sunset Boulevard* on Saturday evening. They (18) _____ (be) both delighted as they loved Andrew Lloyd Webber's music and (19) _____ (try) for ages to get tickets to this particular musical.

It was a perfect evening. They (20) _____ (have) front row seats and the show itself was every bit as good as they (21) _____ (expect). They (22) _____ (be) in

such a good mood after it that they **(23)** _____ (decide) to
go for a meal at their favourite Italian restaurant. When they eventually
(24) _____ (get) home just after midnight, a new shock
(25) _____ (await) them. While they were away, their
house **(26)** _____ (burgle)! Everything of value
(27) _____ (steal). They **(28)** _____ (know)
immediately who the thief was because **(29)** _____ (lie)
on the kitchen table was a note in handwriting they
(30) ——————— (recognize), **(31)** _____ (say):
HOPE YOU **(32)** _____ (enjoy) THE SHOW!

 Read the whole text through first before you decide which tense to use.
Think about **the context** (the rest of the sentence/text), the **time** of the
event and **attitude** (how you view the event). For example, in number 19 the
choices could be 1 *tried*, 2 *were trying*, 3 *had tried* and 4 *had been trying*.
All are possible, but 3 and 4 both indicate the time best (past perfect
because we want to show what had happened before they got the tickets).
Number 4 emphasises how long it can take to get tickets, so, *had been
trying* is the best choice here.

2 Choose the correct verb

Read through the sentences below, then decide which answer, A, B, C or D, best fits each space. There is an example at the beginning (0).

Choose the alternative that fits **grammatically** into the sentence.

0   John _told_ me that he was ill.

     (A) told   **B** explained   **C** said   **D** reported

1   His parents wouldn't _____ him stay out later than 10.30 at night.

     A allow   **B** permit   **C** agree   **D** let

2   The police _____ him for burglary.

     A arrested   **B** charged   **C** convicted   **D** accused

3   Many people _____ about the bad behaviour of soccer fans in the town centre after the match.

     A criticized   **B** disapproved   **C** complained   **D** objected

4   I never wear red. It's a colour that just doesn't _____ me.

     A go with   **B** suit   **C** match   **D** take to

5   See if you can _____ Joe to do his share of the housework.

     A get   **B** have   **C** make   **D** try

6   The train was _____ from leaving because of a signal failure.

     A prevented   **B** forbidden   **C** detained   **D** cancelled

7   After a lot of difficulty he finally _____ to start the car.

     A succeeded   **B** coped   **C** managed   **D** worked out

8   The manager asked her to _____ with the complaint.

     A take care   **B** attend   **C** deal   **D** follow

9 If you want a bank loan, I _____ you to try the National Bank.

A advise   B suggest   C propose   D insist

10 I _____ the meeting to him the other day. I wonder why he didn't turn up.

A mentioned   B warned   C reminded   D pointed

11 Combining our two incomes will _____ us to get a bigger loan from the bank.

A guarantee   B ensure   C enable   D confirm

12 'Did you _____ to put the cat out?'

'I didn't know it was on fire!'

A recall   B remember   C remind   D recollect

13 Is she just _____ to be crazy, or is she really mad?

A imagining   B faking   C asserting   D pretending

14 Am I happy? It all _____ on what you mean by 'happy'!

A includes   B relates   C concerns   D depends

15 I _____ you enjoy the play, Mr Lincoln.

A wish   B hope   C want   D expect

In this kind of test (multiple choice), all the alternatives (A, B, C, D) have similar meanings and are therefore easily confused, but only one fits grammatically. For example, in question 1 you cannot say ~~He explained me that...~~, ~~He said me that...~~ or ~~He reported me that...~~ (You can only say *He explained **to** me that ...*, *He said that ....* [without *me*] and *He reported **to** me that ...*), so only *He told me that ...* is grammatically correct.

3 Phrasal verbs 1: *break, bring, call, come*

A Complete the sentences below with a suitable phrasal verb using *break*. There is an example at the beginning (0).

0 I'm going to have to change my car. It keeps on
___*breaking down*___!

1 The two countries have _____ diplomatic relations.

2 Thieves _____ at the weekend and stole two valuable paintings.

3 Police were called in to _____ the demonstration.

4 The two prisoners _____ from their guards and escaped.

B Complete the sentences below with a suitable phrasal verb using *bring*.

1 It must have been standing in the pouring rain at Saturday's match that _____ your cold.

2 It is far more difficult nowadays to _____ children than it used to be.

3 Gold Software have announced that they are going to _____ thirty new computer games this year.

4 Every time I go camping it _____ happy memories of my youth.

C Complete the sentences below with a suitable phrasal verb using *call*.

1 David said he would _____ us at 7.30 to drive us to the station.

2 Because of objections from local residents they had to _____ the open-air pop concert.

3 If you're visiting Manchester next month, why don't you _____ my sister. She'd be delighted to see you again.

4 They _____ her Emily _____ her grandmother.

D Complete the sentences below with a suitable phrasal verb using *come*.

1 I _____ these old photographs while I was tidying up the attic.

2 It took the boxer over a minute to _____ after he had been knocked out by his opponent.

3 She will _____ quite a lot of money when her grandmother dies.

4 I don't think much of this new washing powder. Look! The stain on my shirt still hasn't _____!

E Without looking back at exercises A–D, write the correct phrasal verb (*break*, *bring*, *call* or *come*) next to the following definitions. (They are in no particular order).

1 collect (someone) (e.g. by car) _____

2 raise (children) _____

3 go and visit (someone) _____

4 appear (e.g. the sun, a flower) _____

5 to stop working, fail mechanically (e.g. a car)

   _____

6 find by accident _____

7 be the cause of, lead to (e.g. a cold) _____

8 enter a building illegally, often with force

   _____

9 cancel _____

10 regain consciousness (after fainting or being knocked out)

   _____

11 recall, cause a memory to return _____

12 inherit (money, property) _____

 The meaning of a phrasal verb can sometimes, but not always, be worked out from the meaning of the particle (preposition or adverb) that follows the verb. For example, the particle *up* is used (amongst other things) to show that an action is completed, as in *Cabbage is good for you, so eat it all up!* i.e. eat all of it.

4 Phrasal verbs 2: *fall, get, go, keep*

A   Complete the sentences below with a suitable phrasal verb using *fall*. There is an example at the beginning (0).

0   The roof of the building _____*fell in*_____, killing two people and injuring twenty others.

1   She slipped and _____, breaking her leg in the process.

2   'I see Paul and Jane aren't speaking to one another.'

'Yes, they've _____ again for some reason.'

3   You didn't _____ that old three-card trick, did you? I didn't think you were so gullible!

4   'Did you get that contract you were talking about?'
'No, it _____.'

B   Complete the sentences below with a suitable phrasal verb using *get*.

1   'When did you _____ from your holidays?'
'Last Friday.'

2   The telephone socket was behind the bookcase which made it very difficult to _____.

3   I tried phoning twice but couldn't _____. The line was engaged each time.

4   All this rain is really _____ me _____. I wish it were summer again.

Section 1: Verbs   9

C   Complete the sentences below with a suitable phrasal verb using *go*.

1   After months of negotiations, the deal finally

_____.

2   Time always seems to _____ so quickly when you're enjoying yourself.

3   Don't drink that milk – it's _____!

4   Do you think this T-shirt will _____ my yellow shorts?

D   Complete the sentences below with a suitable phrasal verb using *keep*.

1   Try to _____ the subject of politics tonight. We don't want Peter and Colin quarrelling again, do we?

2   They were walking so quickly that she found it hard to _____ with them.

3   Do you have any sprays or anything else that will _____ flies and mosquitoes?

4   You haven't told me everything, have you? You're still _____ something _____ .

E Without looking back at exercises A–D, write the correct phrasal verb (*fall*, *get*, *go* or *keep*) next to the following definitions. (They are in no particular order).

1 be connected (by telephone) _____

2 match (style, colour) _____

3 maintain same speed, level as others _____

4 reach (e.g. something on a high shelf) _____

5 be deceived by (e.g. a false story) _____

6 return (e.g. from a holiday) _____

7 withhold (information) _____

8 avoid a subject _____

9 go bad (food, milk) _____

10 depress, demoralise _____

11 quarrel _____

12 pass (time) _____

5 Phrasal verbs 3: *look, put, take*

A Complete the sentences below with a suitable phrasal verb using *look*. There is an example at the beginning (0).

0 Could you _____*look after*_____ the children for me on Friday evening? I've got to go to a Parent-Teacher Association meeting.

1 _____! There's a car coming.

2 Most children _____ to the summer holidays.

3 Do you _____ on your schooldays and think of them as the best days of your life.

4 If you don't know the meaning of a word, _____ it _____ in a dictionary.

5 We've had several complaints this week, Mrs Baker. I'd like you to _____ them please.

B Complete the sentences below with a suitable phrasal verb using *put*.

1 The fire brigade arrived quickly and soon _____ the fire.

2 We've decided to get rid of our coal fires and _____ central heating instead.

3 He tried to _____ some money each week in case of emergencies.

4 By the way, James, there's no meeting tonight after all. It's been _____ until next week.

5 Their dog was old and in pain, so they decided to have it

_____ .

C Complete the sentences below with a suitable phrasal verb using *take*.

1 'Your daughter has a very good voice, Mr Blake.'
'Well, she _____ her mother, not me. I can't
sing a note.'

2 If you want a job, Julie, *The Book Store* are _____
extra staff for Christmas.

3 I tried playing golf once but never really _____
it. As far as I was concerned, it was boring.

4 He sounded so convincing when he said he was a film director
that we were all completely _____ . You can
imagine how surprised we were to learn that in reality he was an
out-of-work plumber.

5 There's a rumour going round that Rainbow Computers are
planning to _____ a top American software
company.

D Without looking back at exercises A–C, write the correct phrasal verb
(*look*, *put* or *take*) next to the following definitions. (They are in no
particular order).

1 examine, investigate (e.g. a complaint) _____

2 develop a liking for (something) _____

3   save (money) _____

4   try to find (information) _____

5   extinguish (a fire) _____

6   gain control of a company _____

7   kill humanely (a pet) _____

8   take care of, care for (someone) _____

9   resemble (in looks, talent) _____

10   remember the past _____

One way to work on your knowledge of phrasal verbs is to draw a matrix like the one below and, using a good EFL dictionary, see how many combinations you can find.

	away	across	down	in	off	up
break	✓					
cut						
give						
keep						
fall						
see						
hold						

6 Phrasal verbs with more than one meaning

Read through the pairs of sentences below, then decide which phrasal verb can be used to replace the words in italics in both. There is an example at the beginning (0).

0 a) I can't decide which dress to *wear*.

b) I *gained* almost a kilo in weight when I was on holiday.

Phrasal verb: _____ put on _____

---

1 a) I *learnt to speak* French when I worked in France one summer.

b) The Prime Minister announced that there were signs that the economy was really *showing signs of recovery*.

Phrasal verb: _____

---

2 a) Are you sure I'm not *inconveniencing* you?

b) It took the fire fighters three hours to *extinguish* the fire.

Phrasal verb: _____

---

3 a) He spoke with such a strong Scottish accent that the students found it really difficult to *understand* what he was saying.

b) I asked him to *write out* the cheque to Celtic Enterprises.

Phrasal verb: _____

---

4 a) When he deliberately punched the other team's goalkeeper, the referee *ordered* him *to leave the field*.

b) Have you *written to them* for their latest catalogue yet?

Phrasal verb: _____

---

5 a) The cost of the new bridge could *reach* millions of pounds.

  b) The car *collided with* a lorry just outside the station.

  Phrasal verb: _____

6 a) You should always *make a copy of* important files on your computer, preferably every day.

  b) If I tell the boss we're not prepared to work overtime this weekend, will the rest of you *support* me?

  Phrasal verb: _____

7 a) I don't think the new fashion will really *become popular.*

  b) He's a bit slow and didn't *realise what was happening* for quite a while.

  Phrasal verb: _____

8 a) She *didn't accept* the job because the salary was too low.

  b) The radio's very loud. *Reduce the volume,* please.

  Phrasal verb: _____

9 a) I shall *decorate and repair* this old house and then sell it.

  b) My hands were so cold that I couldn't *fasten* my top button.

  Phrasal verb: _____

10 a) The old man *donated* half his fortune to charity.

  b) They'll never believe you're French. Your accent will *betray* you.

  Phrasal verb: _____

11 a) They *started their journey* early in the morning to avoid the traffic.

b) The cakes were *arranged* on a trolley, and looked really delicious.

Phrasal verb: _____

12 a) Could you help me to *inflate* these balloons?

b) The partisans *destroyed* the building *with dynamite*.

Phrasal verb: _____

13 a) My father was *summoned to join the army* soon after the war began.

b) How many times have I told you never to *telephone me* at work!

Phrasal verb: _____

14 a) I'm too fat! I'd better *stop eating* biscuits and chocolates.

b) You should always *offer* your seat on a bus to an old or disabled person.

Phrasal verb: _____

15 a) Two masked men *stopped and robbed* a security van and stole over £300,000.

b) The train was *delayed* for two hours because of an accident on the line.

Phrasal verb: _____

 Very often, a phrasal verb has both a literal meaning, e.g., *look up* (into the sky); and a transferred meaning, e.g., *look up* (a word in a dictionary), where *look up* means *search for* or *check*.

7 Confusing verb constructions

Which captions best illustrate the drawings below? Choose from the following and write your answers in the boxes below. There is an example at the beginning.

a He's stopped drinking coffee.

b He's stopped to drink coffee.

c Why don't you try counting sheep?

d Why don't you try to count the sheep?

e She's used to skating.

f She used to skate.

g He's having his hair cut.

h He's cutting his hair.

i Will you marry me?

j Will you be marrying me?

1	2	3	4	5	6	7	8	9	10
c									

3

4

5

6

7

8

9

10

Prepositions

● Prepositions show relationships of various kinds:

Time: *after the show, during the weekend*
Place: *in the garden, under the bridge*
Subject matter: *a book about insects, a lecture on DNA testing*
Opposition: *women against war*
Reaction: *amazed at something*
Means, method: *travel by bus, start by making a list of things to do*
Manner: *with pleasure, without thinking*
Purpose: *I did it for the money, I did it for you*
Origin: *I am from Madrid, made out of old bottles, made of plastic*

● Many expressions involve the use of prepositions:

with verbs: *look after, deal with*
with nouns: *by mistake, out of order*
with adjectives: *allergic to, jealous of*

Note, too, the compound prepositions such as *in spite of, with regard to, by way of.*

'He's allergic to cats.'

8 Prepositional phrases

A Here are thirty words and phrases in alphabetical order. Put them under the correct preposition. Some of them can be used with more than one preposition. There is an example at the beginning.

a change	a diet	a hurry	air	all means	breath
business	date	fire	first	heart	hire	holiday
hospital	instance	last	mistake	~~night~~	once
order	particular	private	purpose	sale	sight
the moment	the ordinary	trouble	work	luck

AT	BY	FOR
night		

IN	ON	OUT OF

B Now complete the following sentences with a suitable prepositional phrase. Choose from the ones above. There is an example at the beginning (0).

0 Owls usually hunt _____*at night*_____. They can see really well in the dark.

1 'May I join you?'
'Yes, _____.'

2 'I hear you're going to Spain. A holiday?'
'No, unfortunately, I have to go there _____.'

3 I've put on nearly three kilos. I think I'd better go _____.

4 I know her _____, but I've no idea what her name is.

5 My uncle had a stroke last week and has been _____ ever since.

6 After running for the bus I was _____.

7 The people at number 10 are emigrating to Australia, so they've put their house up _____.

8 Sorry, Nick, I can't talk just now. I'm _____ but I'll phone you when I get home.

9 Let's go out for a meal tonight _____. I'm fed up with cooking.

10 Mr Grant's very busy _____. Could you come back later?

11 When you saw her on TV she seemed such a nice, kind person, but _____ she was vicious and cruel – especially towards her children.

12 Our teacher made us learn the words of the poem _____.

13 It was an accident I tell you! I certainly didn't drop the vase _____.

14 We'll have to use the stairs. The lift is _____.

15 I've finished my essay _____. It's taken me three hours to do it.

16 I didn't recognize him _____ because he had grown a beard since I last saw him.

All these noun phrases are adverbials, i.e., they say something about the action or state expressed by the verb. For example: *I go by bus* tells you how I travel; *I listened in disbelief* tells you how I listened; *I did it out of habit,* tells you why I did it; *I live in hope* tells you about my mental state.

9 Adjective + preposition

Complete the sentences below with a suitable adjective plus a preposition.
Choose from the following. Some of the prepositions will be used more than
once. There is an example at the beginning (0).

absent	absorbed	cruel	eligible	famous	~~fond~~
friendly	good	grateful	ill	jealous	keen
proud	responsible	rich	satisfied	serious	
short	similar	terrified			

about	at	for	from	in	of	on	to	with

0 Both my dogs are very _____*fond of*_____ ice cream.

1 I've been _____ a cold for over a week.

2 I've always been _____ water ever since I nearly
drowned as a child.

3 Mark's been _____ school for over a month.
He'll have a lot of catching up to do when he comes back.

4 Our daughter has just graduated as a doctor. We are very
_____ her.

5 Could I phone you later, Alan? I'm a bit _____
time right now.

6 Costa Rica is _____ its beautiful scenery.

7 My cousin is very _____ music and can play
four or five instruments.

8   I like ballet but I'm not very _____ opera.

9   Julie's my oldest friend. We've been _____ one another since we were at Primary school.

10   There's no pleasing our teacher. He's never _____ our work!

11   For the last time, who is _____ this mess?

12   We are _____ you for all you've done for us.

13   I'm afraid only single people under the age of thirty are _____ membership of this club.

14   Michael was _____ his sister's success, even though he pretended to be happy for her.

15   She is _____ her sister in character.

16   Australia is _____ natural resources.

17   He was so _____ what he was doing that he didn't notice me come into the room.

18   Small children are often _____ animals without realizing it. They don't mean to hurt them.

19   You're not _____ leaving this country and going to live in China, are you?

 In the case of adjectives ending in -ed (i.e. formed from verbs), more than one preposition might be used, with only a slight difference of meaning, e.g., *worried by your attitude, worried about you.*

10 Verb + preposition

Complete the sentences below with a suitable verb plus a preposition. Choose from the following and make any necessary changes. Some of the prepositions will be used more than once. There is an example at the beginning (0).

apologize	arrive	believe	care	charge
compliment	feel sorry	insure	lose	prefer
protect	rely	remind	share	smell	succeed
suffer	think	translate	~~write~~	

about	against	among	at	by	for	from
in	into	of	on	to	with	

0   Hamlet was _____*written by*_____ Shakespeare.

1   This book has been _____ five languages, including Russian.

2   The man was arrested and _____ murder.

3   After three attempts she finally _____ breaking the world record.

4   'Does Mark really _____ flying saucers?' 'Oh yes, he's quite convinced they exist.'

5   'Does Peter _____ you _____ Michael Jackson?' 'No, he doesn't look anything like him!'

6   'May I _____ you _____ your wonderful garden?' 'This isn't my garden. I live in that house over there!'

7   It was largely my fault that we _____ tennis. I played so badly.

8   We left Heathrow airport at 16.45 and _____
    Copenhagen at 19.30.

9   Don't forget to wear a scarf. It will _____ you
    _____ the cold.

10 You should always _____ your home
    _____ fire.

11 The mother told the group of children to _____
    the sweets _____ themselves.

12 Although she had only painted the kitchen, the whole flat
    _____ paint.

13 My sister _____ hay fever every summer.

14 I really _____ people who are tone deaf. It
    must be awful not to be able to sing.

15 If I were you Julie, I'd _____ very carefully
    _____ his offer. I don't think you'll get a better
    one.

16 She made the children _____ their bad
    behaviour at the party.

17 'Would you _____ another piece of cake, Frank?'
    'No, thanks, Jill. I really couldn't eat another thing.'

18 Most young people _____ pop music
    _____ classical music.

19 Ask Mike to do it. You can _____ him. He
    never lets you down.

Some words can be either a preposition or an adverb, e.g. *across, down, in,
on*, etc. Remember that the object will always follow a preposition, but may
come between a verb and an adverb, as in *get across the road* (preposition)
compared with *get an idea across* (adverb).

11 Verb + noun + preposition

Combine the verbs and prepositions with nouns from the middle column to make useful fixed expressions. There are examples at the beginning (0) and (00).

verb	noun	preposition
catch find have keep make pay take	0 confidence 00 contact 1 eyes 2 faith 3 fault 4 friends 5 fun 6 issue 7 offence 8 pleasure 9 pride 10 exception 11 attention 12 advantage 13 sight 14 track 15 provision	at for in of to with

Write your answers here:

0	_have_ confidence _in_
00	_make_ contact _with_
1	___ ___ ___
2	___ ___ ___
3	___ ___ ___
4	___ ___ ___
5	___ ___ ___
6	___ ___ ___
7	___ ___ ___
8	___ ___ ___
9	___ ___ ___
10	___ ___ ___
11	___ ___ ___
12	___ ___ ___
13	___ ___ ___
14	___ ___ ___
15	___ ___ ___

Now use six of the expressions to complete the following sentences.

16   It's good to _____ _____ _____ your
      appearance, but try not to be vain!

17   There are so many developments in computer technology
      nowadays, I just can't _____ _____ _____
      them all.

18   Please _____ _____ _____ everything I
      say, because I shall say it only once. Understood?

19   My daughter found it easy to _____ _____
      _____ other children, but my son was very shy and was
      mostly alone.

20   Our English teacher is nice because she praises us a lot, but most
      of the other teachers seem to _____ _____
      _____ everything we do.

21   You want cut-price DVDs? Then _____ _____
      _____ our bargain offers. At least 30% off list price!!

It is important to learn these expressions by heart, and in particular to be
careful not to insert an article between verb and noun. For example, use the
expression *catch sight of* and people will be impressed by your command of
English, but if you say *catch the sight of*, it will spoil the effect!

12 Compound prepositions

Combine the nouns from the middle column with prepositions to make useful fixed expressions. There are two examples at the beginning (0) and (00).

preposition	noun	preposition
at by in on out of under with for	0 account 00 addition 1 agreement 2 answer 3 behalf 4 common 5 exchange 6 favour 7 good terms 8 love 9 means 10 odds 11 pity 12 reference 13 the compliments 14 the expense 15 the influence 16 the sake	for of to with

Write your answers here:

0	__on__ account __of__
00	__in__ addition __to__
1	__ __ __
2	__ __ __
3	__ __ __
4	__ __ __
5	__ __ __
6	__ __ __
7	__ __ __
8	__ __ __
9	__ __ __
10	__ __ __
11	__ __ __
12	__ __ __
13	__ __ __
14	__ __ __
15	__ __ __
16	__ __ __

Now use six of the expressions to complete the following sentences.

17   Dear Sirs

_____ your enquiry of June 15, we are unable to supply the goods you requested ...

18   It's a good idea to remain _____ your neighbours. Bad feelings between neighbours can make life hell for everyone!

19   _____ your question: 'No, I am not going to a fancy dress party; I always dress like this.'

20   People who drive _____ drugs or alcohol are a danger to themselves and to everyone else.

21   'Mummy, what do humans have _____ apes?'

'Well, dear, judging by your father, I'd say they were both hairy and scratch a lot.'

22   Sometimes, couples who really ought to split up will stay together _____ the children.

Some of these compound prepositions are used in everyday speech, e.g., *in favour* of. However, many of them are formal written expressions, for which there is an everyday equivalent, e.g. A teacher is more likely to say *I want to speak to you about your work* rather than *I want to speak to you with regard to your homework.*

13 Question words

These questions are taken from a General Knowledge Quiz. Fill in the missing question words below, all of which begin with a preposition. Then choose the correct answer to the question, A, B or C. There is an example at the beginning (0).

0 _In which_ year did the first man land on the moon?

(A) 1968　　　　B 1969　　　　C 1970

1 _____ city were the 1996 Olympic Games held?

A Atlanta　　　B Sydney　　　C Barcelona

2 _____ name was St. Petersburg formerly known?

A Moscow　　　B Leningrad　　　C Murmansk

3 _____ section of the orchestra does the 'trumpet' belong?

A percussion　　　B brass　　　C woodwind

4 _____ part of the body would you find 'the bridge'?

A the ear　　　B the foot　　　C the nose

5 _____ language does the word 'sauna' originate?

A Swedish　　　B Norwegian　　　C Finnish

6 _____ country do you associate baseball?

A Britain　　　B Australia　　　C the United States

7 _____ century was the Taj Mahal in India built?

A 17th　　　B 16th　　　C 15th

8 _____ country would you associate the dish 'couscous'?

    A Greece   **B** Tunisia   **C** South Korea

9 _____ foot was the Prince able to fit the glass slipper?

    A Cinderella's   **B** Rapunzel's   **C** Griselda's

10 _____ country did Columbus sail for 'the Indies'?

    A Spain   **B** Italy   **C** Portugal

11 _____ kind of music is New Orleans famous?

    A jazz   **B** reggae   **C** country and western

12 _____ way does an Indian elephant differ from an African elephant?

    A It has smaller ears.   **B** It lives on curry.   **C** It is brown not grey.

13 _____ part of the world is Spanish spoken (apart from Spain)?

    A Brazil   **B** Indonesia   **C** Mexico

14 _____ head did William Tell place the apple?

    A his son's   **B** the King's   **C** Herr Bircher Muesli's

Prepositions frequently occur at the end of a sentence, as in **Where** *are you* **from**? or *I don't know* **what** *the world is coming* **to**. Nobody would say *From where are you?* or *To what is the world coming?* Similarly, people say *Who are you talking about?* rather than *About whom are you talking?* (although the latter is correct, of course).

14 Particles and prepositions

Fill in the missing prepositions or adverb particles in the following passage. There is an example at the beginning (0).

THE CURSE OF TUTANKHAMUN

Most people scoff **(0)** _____at_____ the idea of curses coming true, but the events that followed the opening **(1)** _____ Tutankhamun's tomb **(2)** _____ Howard Carter **(3)** _____ 1922 may make them think twice **(4)** _____ laughing.

The story **(5)** _____ the curse began when the last man climbed out **(6)** _____ the tomb. It is said that a sudden sandstorm blew **(7)** _____ and that the men **(8)** _____ the party saw a hawk, the ancient royal symbol **(9)** _____ Egypt, fly overhead.

Local Egyptians took this to mean that the spirit **(10)** _____ the dead king had left his tomb, cursing those who had opened it. Five months later, the man who financed the expedition, Lord Caernarvon, was bitten **(11)** _____ the cheek **(12)** _____ a mosquito. Normally nothing too serious! But the bite became infected and Caernarvon caught pneumonia and died **(13)** _____ an Egyptian hospital.

(14) _____ the precise moment **(15)** _____ his death, all the lights **(16)** _____ Cairo went **(17)** _____ , and thousands **(18)** _____ miles away **(19)** _____ the Caernarvon mansion **(20)** _____ Hampshire, England, his dog began to howl – and died **(21)** _____ the night. Doctors who examined the mummified body **(22)** _____ Tutankhamun reported that he had a small depression **(23)** _____ his cheek, just like a mosquito bite, **(24)** _____ exactly the same spot where Caernarvon had been bitten.

Many people who visited the tomb also died **(25)** _____
strange circumstances. Lord Caernarvon's half brother died
(26) _____ a burst appendix. An Egyptian prince whose family
claimed they were descended **(27)** _____ the pharaohs was
murdered **(28)** _____ London and his brother committed
suicide. An American railway tycoon caught a cold while
(29) _____ the tomb and died **(30)** _____ pneumonia.

The man who helped Howard Carter to catalogue the items
found **(31)** _____ the tomb committed suicide, and a
few months later his father jumped **(32)** _____ his death
(33) _____ the balcony **(34)** _____ his London flat.
There was an alabaster vase **(35)** _____ the tomb
(36) _____ the room that he jumped
(37) _____ (*two words*).

(38) _____ 1966 the government **(39)** _____
Egypt agreed to lend the treasures **(40)** _____ France
(41) _____ an important exhibition. The Director
(42) _____ the Antiquities fought **(43)** _____ the
decision, because he had dreamed that he would die if he allowed the
treasures to go **(44)** _____ (*2 words*) Egypt. When he left the
last meeting, still trying to make the authorities change their minds, he
was knocked down **(45)** _____ a car and died two days later.

And Howard Carter who was the first man **(46)** _____
the tomb? He died – **(47)** _____ natural causes –
(48) _____ 1939.

Sentence construction

The two most important elements in sentence construction in English are sequence of tenses and word order.

- Sequence of tenses

The meaning changes depending on the tense used, e.g.:

If you hadn't given him the money, he wouldn't have gone to South America. (he's already gone)

If you hadn't given him the money, he wouldn't be going to South America next week. (he hasn't gone yet)

I wish you wouldn't do that. (you are doing something I disapprove of)

I wish you hadn't done that (you did something I disapprove of)

- Word order

It is clear that *The dog bit the man* is different from *The man bit the dog*, but what about the difference between [1] *He carefully opened the box* and [2] *He opened the box carefully*? or between [3] *Let's meet on Friday at 12 o'clock* and [4] *Let's meet at 12 o'clock on Friday*? Whatever comes at the beginning or end of the phrase (called front focus and end focus) is emphasised. So, sentence [1] simply states a fact, whereas [2] draws our attention to **how** he opened the box, i.e. carefully; sentence [3] draws your attention to the TIME (i.e. 12 o'clock), and sentence [4] highlights which DAY we should meet (i.e. Friday).

'If you hadn't given him the money, he wouldn't be going to South America.'

15 Position of adjectives and adverbs

A Put the adjectives in the correct places and in the right order in the following sentences. There is an example at the beginning (0).

0 She bought a handbag in the sale. (leather, brown)
She brought a brown leather handbag in the sale.

1 He bought a bunch of roses. (yellow, sweet-smelling)

_____

2 The nextdoor neighbour's cat has soft fur. (grey, lovely)

_____

3 The hotel was owned by a businessman. (tall, German, middle-aged)

_____

4 They lived in a house. (three-bedroomed, semi-detached, brand new)

_____

5 My brother loves sports cars. (red, Italian, fast)

_____

6 In the middle of the room was a coffee table. (oval, superb, oak)

_____

7 Where did you get this vase from? (old, magnificent, Japanese)

_____

8 I love meals. (tasty, hot, Indian)

_____

9   He was wearing a jacket. (shabby, cream, old, linen)

_____

10   Outside the Town Hall was a statue. (marble, huge, triangular, black)

_____

B   Put the adverbs in the best places in the following sentences. There is an example at the beginning (0).

0   We have a lie-in on Sunday morning. (usually)
We usually have a lie-in on Sunday morning.
_____

1   The children go riding on Saturdays. (sometimes)

_____

2   I was pretending. I wouldn't have chopped your finger off! (only, really)

_____

3   Carol's daughter plays the violin. (beautifully)

_____

4   My brother finishes work on Fridays. (nearly always, early)

_____

5   I don't go to the theatre. My sister, on the other hand, goes. (often, regularly)

_____

6   I don't understand why Joanna didn't want to come to my party. (still)

_____

7 George hasn't done much work so he'll fail the exam. (probably)

_____

8 I disagree with you! Watching football live is better than watching it on TV. (completely, definitely)

_____

9 'Where's Rose?'
'She's gone home.' (just)

_____

10 'Is my omelette ready?' (yet)
'No, dear, I'm waiting for the hen to lay the eggs!' (still)

_____

Adjectives usually go in this order:

1 Value   2 Size   3 Age/Temperature   4 Shape   5 Colour   6 Origin
7 Material

Rather than trying to remember that order (and it is unusual to have more than three adjectives together anyway), it is better to remember a few key phrases, e.g.

a	beautiful	old	Chinese	vase
	value	age	origin	

a	huge	black	metal	box
	size	colour	material	

16 *If*-clauses

A Complete the clauses 1–15 with a suitable clause from those marked a–p. Write your answers in the boxes on the next page. There is an example at the beginning (0).

0 She'll have to wait in my room ...

1 I'll have to sell my car ...

2 You'd feel a lot better ...

3 We would have caught the last bus ...

4 You'll lose quite a lot of weight ...

5 He'll probably pass his exams ...

6 She won't be able to go to university ...

7 We would have had a picnic this afternoon ...

8 I'd ask her to marry me ...

9 He told us he wouldn't go on working ...

10 You'll fail your exams ...

11 The firm wouldn't have gone bankrupt ...

12 I'll drive you to the station ...

13 I'd lend you the money ...

14 You'd make a better impression at the interview ...

15 The match will go to extra time ...

a ... unless she passes her A-levels.

b ... if I wasn't so broke myself.

c ... unless one of the teams scores soon.

d ... if he keeps on working hard.

e ... if you cut your hair and wore a suit.

f	... if I thought she'd say yes.
g	... if you gave up smoking.
h	... if I can borrow mum's car.
i	... unless you work harder.
j	... if you go jogging every day.
k	... unless I get a job soon.
l	... if they hadn't tried to expand so quickly.
m	... if it hadn't rained.
n	... if we hadn't stayed for that last drink.
o	... if he won a lot of money.
p	... if she arrives before I get back from lunch.

0	1	2	3	4	5	6	7	8	9	10	11	12	13	14	15
p															

B Now complete the sentences below using the correct tense of the verbs in brackets. Add any other words that may be necessary. There is an example at the beginning (0).

0 We will have to cancel the concert tomorrow if it
doesn't stop raining . (rain)

1 'If you were my wife, I _____
a big dose of poison.' (give)

'If you were my husband, I _____ it!' (drink)

2 If I lend you the money, _____
me back next week?   (pay)

3 If you had been more careful, the accident
_____ .   (not happen)

4 He _____ with us unless his
brother comes too.   (not come)

5 If _____, they would have
cancelled the concert.   (rain)

6 She _____ the match unless
she plays better.   (lose)

7 I _____ the job if I had known
it was going to be so badly paid.   (not take)

8 If you _____ harder, you'd
soon be able to play the guitar well.   (practise)

9 The accident wouldn't have happened if you
_____ so fast.   (not drive)

- Unreal conditionals are those which describe an impossible or unfulfilled condition, and then describe the consequences:
  If the Queen were a man, she would be King.

- There is also the conditional which describes not what **is**, but what **might have been**. It is often used to express regret:
  If I hadn't gone to the disco, I wouldn't have lost my teeth in a fight.

- Note these two similar constructions:
  *If you **add** water to copper sulphate, it **turns** blue.* (i.e., *if* here means *every time you do it*)

  *If you **kiss** me, I **will tell** my mother.* (i.e. my telling is conditional on your kissing me)

17 Ambiguous wording

The following newspaper extracts, headlines, etc. are written in such a way that there is an extra, unexpected meaning to the one that was intended – often with amusing results. Explain the 'other' meaning. There is an example at the beginning (0).

0   Dear milkman, Baby arrived yesterday. Please leave another.
Unexpected meaning: Please leave another baby.

1   It is bad manners to break your bread and roll in your soup.

_____

2   Angry bull injures farmer with a gun.

_____

3   Dog for sale: eats anything and is very fond of children.

_____

4   West End Theatre is looking for actors and actresses to perform in a play dealing with the effects of drugs. Experience preferred.

_____

5   Busy seaside restaurant requires man to wash dishes and two waitresses.

_____

6   The Queen named the ship as she slid gently into the water.

_____

7   The motorist involved in the accident declared that the other driver smelled of drink. So did a policeman.

_____

8   WANTED: zinc bath for adult with strong bottom.

_____

18 Conjunctions

A Complete the clauses 1–15 with a suitable clause from those marked a–p. Write your answers in the boxes on the next page. There is an example at the beginning (0).

0 Use microwaveable food ...

1 He promised to give his parents a call ...

2 I wouldn't take a job there ...

3 As a child, she wasn't allowed to go to bed ...

4 You can borrow the car ...

5 He never went abroad on holiday ...

6 We'll have a picnic this afternoon ...

7 Take a jumper with you ...

8 I always feel like singing ...

9 Everyone in the room went completely quiet ...

10 She couldn't go to the party ...

11 She'll be a very good reporter ...

12 She confessed that she married her husband ...

13 I won't pass my exams in the summer ...

14 The Board meeting should be over by four o'clock ...

15 I'll go to the party with you tonight ...

a ... even if they offered me £5,000 a month.

b ... once she's had more experience.

c ... whenever I hear that song on the radio.

d ... even though she didn't love him at the time.

e ... assuming there's nothing controversial on the agenda.

f	... because she was ill.
g	... until she had kissed everyone goodnight.
h	... as the headmaster stood up to announce the exam results.
i	... so that you won't need to spend ages cooking things.
j	... in case it gets colder later on.
k	... as soon as he got to his hotel.
l	... although he could easily afford it.
m	... provided that the weather stays fine.
n	... if you pick me up from work.
o	... unless I work a lot harder.
p	... as long as you fill it up with petrol.

0	1	2	3	4	5	6	7	8	9	10	11	12	13	14	15
i															

B Now complete the sentences below with a suitable conjunction. Choose from the ones found in (A).

1 Of course you can borrow my CDs, _____ you bring them back.

2 Everyone started cheering _____ the band came on stage.

3 Take an umbrella with you _____ it rains.

4 Nobody leaves this kitchen _____ I find out who put the cat in the refrigerator.

5   I was blamed for the accident, _____ it wasn't my fault.

6   You'll enjoy skating _____ you've got the hang of it.

7   He won't play for our club _____ we pay him.

8   We didn't go on holiday this year _____ we couldn't afford it.

9   _____ you don't try, then how do you know you can't do it?

10   I wouldn't go out with her _____ she was the last woman on earth!

Conjunctions show relationships between sentences and clauses, e.g., *reason*, as in *I am tired **because** I have worked too hard*; *purpose*, as in *Do it now **so** that you can relax later*. There are a few compound conjunctions: ***As far as** I know, David is in Bahia; It's all right to surf the net **as long as** you don't spend all your time at the computer.*

19 Word order

Rearrange the words in the sentences below to form twelve correct questions. (Add capital letters, question marks and other punctuation marks where necessary.) There is an example at the beginning (0).

0 the train when last does leave
When does the last train leave?

1 know Mariarosa do here you works if

2 you way tell station me could to excuse the please me the

3 tickets performance are for *Aida* there Saturday's any of left not

4 you how from often borrow do the library books

5 post did I you that you gave remember letter to

6 switch night which the to before of light went you off forgot bed to last you

7 your you not with I to toes if me promise step will dance on

8 interested of tennis a weekend are game in either of this you playing

9 sometimes is what do about all you life wonder

10   there day of the is tomorrow chance off having any

_____

11   been South country any ever to you American Brazil have or other

_____

12   the can on what a coffee leave time it and does you get bus

_____

Word order can change to place emphasis on some part of the sentence, e.g. _I usually get up at six o'clock_ simply states a fact, but _Usually, I get up at six o'clock_ prepares us for a completion like ... _but lately I have been getting up much later._ Where no particular emphasis is required, the usual adverbial order is manner (how), place (where) and time (when), e.g. _He slipped quietly out of the house just after midnight._

20 What's the question?

Rewrite the following questions to ask about the words in bold type. There is an example at the beginning (0).

0 The ring cost £200,000.
How much did the ring cost?

1 She sees her sister **three times a week**.

_____

2 Karen's husband works in **Singapore**.

_____

3 Paul weighs **seventy-five kilos**.

_____

4 The team plays football **at least three times a week**.

_____

5 David has lived in Australia **since 1992**.

_____

6 The group had to wait **ages** to get through customs.

_____

7 The family finally got home last night **at 11.30**.

_____

8 Jill has **bright red** hair.

_____

9 Sam bought **three** pairs of shoes in the sales.

_____

10 **Peter's** brother is a famous soccer player.

_____

11   He paid for the goods **with a credit card**.

_____

12   San Diego is **about two hours** by car from LA.

_____

13   She met her boyfriend **at an open-air pop concert**.

_____

14   He only has **coffee** for breakfast.

_____

15   They arrested him **for shoplifting**.

_____

16   My mother spoke **Italian** fluently as a child.

_____

17   This pen once belonged to **his great grandfather**.

_____

18   **Jane** has a white sports car.

_____

Remember that the word after the question word is always part of the verb.
Where there is an auxiliary (*have, is*, etc.) or modal (*can, should*, etc.) that
goes after the question-word: *Where* **have** *you been*? *What* **can** *you tell
me*? In the case of the simple tenses, you have to 'supply' an auxiliary, that
is, *do, does* or *did*: e.g., **He went** becomes **Where did he go**? Avoid the
common mistakes such as ~~Where he went~~? and ~~Where did he went~~?

21 Choose the best phrase

Read through the following newspaper article and then choose the best phrase from the list (a–o) given below to fill each gap. There is an example at the beginning (0).

Smoking 'will kill one million young people'

PROLONGED smoking will kill around one million British teenagers and children in middle age (0) __e__ , says a report published yesterday.

A further one million will die of tobacco-related diseases in old age, (1) _____ at the Imperial Cancer Research Fund and the World Health Organisation. On present trends, 4–5 million young Britons (2) _____ .

Professor Richard Peto, of the ICRF, said that worldwide somebody (3) _____ which was already killing three million people each year, and the number was increasing.

'In most countries (4) _____ . If current smoking patterns persist, then by the time the young smokers of today (5) _____ there will be about ten million deaths a year from tobacco – one every three seconds. Furthermore, young people continue to see misleading portrayals (6) _____ . It tells them that lighting up is acceptable. It is

no surprise therefore that 90 per cent of smokers start when young.'

He argued that (7) _____ about the effects of prolonged smoking, because of the very long delay between cause and effect. The risk came decades later.

'If cigarette smokers start young and don't stop, about half will be killed by tobacco.' This means that the developing countries (8) _____ , said Professor Peto.

Dr Alan Lopez of the World Health Organisation in Geneva, added: 'The WHO has called on governments everywhere to protect children from (9) _____ . The sooner tobacco advertising is banned, the more lives will be saved.'

Professor Sir Richard Doll – one of the two people (10) _____ forty years ago – urged the Government to increase tax on cigarettes and ban advertising.

'It is quite incredible they don't do it. Here you have something that (11) _____ and people are being encouraged to do it. It is immoral, there is no other word for it.'

a	of smoking as romantic and sporting
b	who proved the link between smoking and lung cancer
c	there has been widespread misunderstanding
d	there has been little notice paid
e	if current patterns continue
f	is killing one sixth of the population prematurely
g	are sitting on a time bomb
h	the worst is yet to come
i	it is both cruel and deadly
j	according to the report by scientists
k	the advertising and promotion of tobacco
l	died every ten seconds through smoking
m	reach middle or old age
n	will become regular smokers
o	refusal to ban tobacco advertising

Sources of confusion (similar words and structures)

There are several causes of confusion, usually because of interference from our mother tongue:

- One word in English, for two words in another language, e.g. *be* in English, *ser* and *estar* in Spanish.

- Two words in English for one word in another language, e.g. *make* and *do* in English, *fare* in Italian.

- The same idea expressed in different ways in the two languages, e.g., *I read a book last night* could be *chital* or *prochital* in Russian depending on whether I just read part of it or read the whole book from cover to cover.

- False friends (*faux amis* in French), that is, words which are similar in appearance but which mean something different or are used in a different way: *eventual* (English) is not the same as *eventuel* (German); *control* (English) is not the same as *controllare* (Italian); *office* (English) is not the same as *ofis* (Turkish) and so on.

- Presence or absence of grammatical features, e.g. the definite article (*the*) and when to omit it. This is a nightmare for people whose language does not have a definite article (e.g. Russian, Turkish), or who have something very like the English definite article, but who use it very differently (e.g. Arabic).

- Singular and plural differences. For example, *people* and *police* are plural in English but singular in many other languages. *Information* and *advice* are singular in English, but plural in many other languages.

22 The definite and indefinite article

In the following sentences put in *a/an* or *the*, but only where necessary. There is an example at the beginning (0).

0 First of all we went to ___—___ Lake Garda and then we went walking in ___*the*___ Alps.

1 _____ Isle of Wight is _____ island off _____ south coast of _____ England.

2 Would you like to see _____ picture of _____ village I lived in when I was _____ child?

3 _____ President of _____ United States lives in _____ White House in _____ Washington D.C.

4 _____ Nelson's Column is in _____ Trafalgar Square, quite near _____ National Gallery.

5 Her brother is _____ musician. He plays _____ flute in _____ orchestra. He has been doing this since he left _____ school at _____ age of eighteen.

6 _____ Doctor Williams works in _____ large hospital in _____ North Wales, near _____ coast.

7 Shall we go for _____ walk in _____ Hyde Park this afternoon or shall we go and see _____ Van Gogh exhibition at _____ Tate Gallery instead?

8 'Do British people shake _____ hands when they meet?' 'Yes, sometimes, but not as often as _____ Swedes do.'

9   My sister lives in _____ old house in _____ Barton
    Place. She's got _____ small flat there on _____ top
    floor.

10 What _____ awful weather! I thought you said
    _____ French Riviera was always hot and sunny.
    _____ rain and storms of _____ past few days are
    more typical of _____ Britain than _____
    Mediterranean.

'Awful weather'

23 Infinitive or *-ing* form?

Complete the sentences below with a suitable verb, using either the infinitive (*to buy*, *to come*, etc.) or the -ing form (*buying*, *coming*, etc.). Choose from the following and use each verb once only. There are two examples at the beginning (0 and 00).

be	~~buy~~	~~come~~	find	get	give	hurt	leave
like	live	meet	play	save	see	stay	take
	talk	teach	think	walk	want	win	

0   Remember _____**to buy**_____ some milk on your way home tonight.

00   I'm busy at the moment. Would you mind _____**coming**_____ back later?

1   I'm sorry, Joe. I didn't mean _____ your feelings.

2   When she was a child, her parents wouldn't allow her _____ in the street.

3   There must be something wrong with Simon. He keeps _____ he's being followed by a private detective.

4   As they'd received a bomb threat, the police ordered everyone _____ the building.

5   What with inflation and everything, it's just not worth _____ nowadays.

6   I remember _____ to be a pop star when I was a child.

7   Don't pretend _____ jazz. I know you hate it really.

8   'Sara hasn't got a car. Would you mind _____ her a lift?'
'No, not at all.'

9 I really enjoy going to parties and _____ new people.

10 Her parents were very strict and wouldn't allow her _____ out later than 10.30.

11 Parents usually warn their children against _____ to strangers.

12 I never go swimming because I dislike _____ my hair wet.

13 I agreed _____ her English if she helped me with my Spanish.

14 It was a very tough match, but in the end England managed _____ by two goals to one.

15 He suggested _____ a taxi to the station.

16 The film star disguised herself to avoid _____ recognized.

17 Would you dare _____ through a graveyard on your own at night?

18 She was very upset when she failed _____ work in Sydney.

19 He wasn't happy with his room so he demanded _____ the manager.

20 It's hard to imagine _____ without television, isn't it? What on earth would you do in the evenings?

In some cases, we use either the *to*-infinitive or the *-ing* form, but with a change of meaning. *This stone is really heavy:* **try** *to* **lift** *it*, as against *If you have hiccups,* **try** *holding your breath.* Sometimes the difference is very small: [1] *I* **like to cook** *Indian food when my friends come for dinner*, as against [2] *I like* **cooking Indian meals** *for friends*. In sentence [1], I am thinking about individual occasions when I cook for my friends; in sentence [2] I am thinking about a general habit that I have.

24 Common mistakes

A There is a wrong word in each of the following sentences. Replace with the correct word. There is an example at the beginning (0).

0 George and (me) would like to invite you to our going-away party.
_____*I*_____

1 Anybody knows what happened to the Marie Celeste. It's a complete mystery. _____

2 I have few time to spare before my flight leaves; let's go and have a coffee. _____

3 My three cousins passed the entrance examination. Both of them are at university now. _____

4 As a child, I used to being on my own a lot. _____

5 There are less birds about than there were when I was young.
_____

6 The twins passed the entrance examination. All of them are at university now. _____

7 My parents played the piano, but none of them could read music.
_____

8 You won't find many money in my purse! _____

9 After picking a bunch of grapes, I ate few and put the rest in a basket. _____

10 The birthday card was signed 'With love from George and I'. _____

11 As a child, I was used to be on my own a lot. _____

12 All of us played the piano, but neither of us could read music.
_____

13 You won't find much pound coins in my purse! _____

14 I have any time to spare for such nonsense; I am far too busy.
_____

15 Nobody can tell you where Big Ben is. It's easy to find. _____

B The underlined word(s) are wrong. Replace with the correct word or words. There is an example at the beginning (0).

0 The relationship between a dog and <u>it's</u> owner can be very close.
   _____*its*_____

16 I won't tell you my problems: you've got enough problems of <u>yours</u>. _____

17 I wonder <u>whose</u> playing this weekend? _____

18 I've got enough problems, I don't need to listen to <u>your own</u>.

   _____

19 I wonder <u>who's</u> pen this is. _____

20 Go to the shop and get me a <u>matchbox</u>: I want to set fire to the Town Hall. _____

21 A fox would not make a good pet because <u>its</u> wild and difficult to control. _____

Some of the mistakes in these sentences are made by native speakers too! Particular examples are:
- saying ~~Come with my friend and I~~ instead of *my friend and me* and vice versa. People who are not sure which is correct will say *my friend and myself* instead.
- saying *less* instead of *fewer* with plural nouns: ~~less calories~~ instead of *fewer calories*.
- in writing, confusing *its* and *it's*.

25 Confusing pairs

Which captions best illustrate the drawings below? Choose from the following and write your answers in the boxes below. There is an example at the beginning.

a   Throw the ball to Charlie!

b   Throw the ball at Charlie!

c   Pass me a knife, please.

d   Pass me the knife, please.

e   Look at those two talking to themselves.

f   Look at those two talking to each other.

g   She likes chocolate more than me.

h   She likes chocolate more than I do.

i   The man is boring.

j   The man is bored.

1	2	3	4	5	6	7	8	9	10
g									

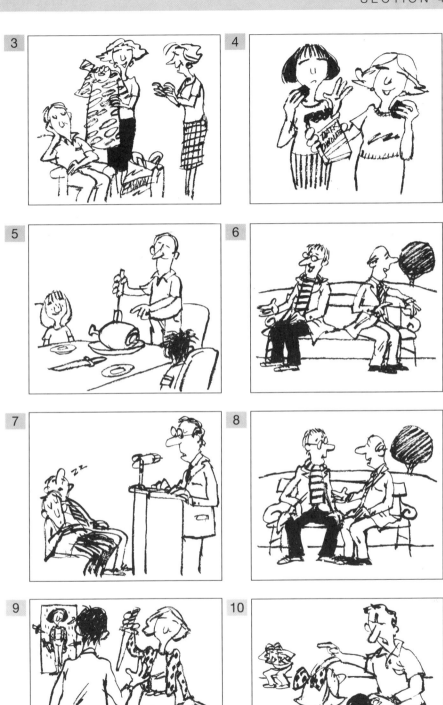

26 Use of *some* and *any*

Complete the following sentences using *some* or *any*, or words beginning with *some* and *any* (something, anyone, etc.). There is an example at the beginning (0).

0 'Who were you talking to?'
'Oh, it wasn't _____*anyone*_____ you know.'

1 My uncle has so much money. I wish he'd give me
_____ as I never seem to have _____ .

2 '_____'s been reading my mail!'
'Well, don't look at me. I haven't been _____ near
the office all day!'

3 '_____ to declare, Sir?'
'Well, I bought _____ perfume for my wife, but they
told me in the shop I wouldn't have to pay _____
duty on it.'

4 Why don't you bring _____ of your friends to the
party? Unless you're doing _____ else of course.

5 Most people don't have _____ idea of how serious
the present economic crisis is. If the Government don't do
_____ soon to bring down unemployment then
they're not going to have _____ choice but to put
up taxes again.

6 'But there must be _____ biscuits left! I bought a
whole packet yesterday.'
'_____ must have eaten them, then, because there
definitely aren't _____ left in the tin.'

7 'I feel like going out _____ this weekend.'
'_____ in particular?'
'No, not really. I just need to do _____ different for change.'

8 'Did you go _____ last night?'
'No, we had _____ friends round for a meal.'

9 'Can I help you?'
'Yes, I'd like _____ information about trains from London to Edinburgh, please. Are there _____ early in the morning?'

10 We haven't got _____ milk. Pop out and get _____, would you, please?

11 These, without _____ doubt, are _____ of the biggest pumpkins I have ever seen. They should definitely win first prize in the Garden Show.

The simple rule that *some* is used with positive statements, and *any* is used with negatives is a good one: *I need some money, I haven't got any money.* Remember that words like *hardly* and *scarcely* are also negative: *I scarcely had any time left to eat anything.*
In questions, we use *any* if we are just asking for information: *Is there any cake left?* But sometimes a question is really an invitation or a request, in which case we would probably use *some*, as in *Would you like some more tea? Would somebody please help me load the car?*

27 Choose the best word

Choose the word which best fits each gap. There is an example at the beginning (0).

Miss Darby lived alone in a large Victorian house **(0)** *in* the road

$$\boxed{over}$$

on

from us. Mother said that Miss Darby was **(1)** *one* of those people who

some

any

never threw **(2)** *something* away. Although I had **(3)** *never* been in her

nothing

anything

even

often

house, I knew that all the rooms were stuffed with furniture and

bric-a-brac of **(4)** *each* kind. I knew this, because her cleaning lady

every

all

(5) *use* to come over to our house sometimes **(6)** *to* a cup of tea and a

used

uses

as

for

chat with my mother. I once heard her **(7)** *to describes* the huge

describing

to describe

bundles of newspapers and goodness knows what **(8)** *else* that cluttered

other

more

the house. When Miss Darby died, her twin nephews came to clear out

the house. The nephews **(9)** *hired* a furniture removal company to take

took

lent

away all the good furniture and paintings, while they **(10)** *went*

did

made

repeated trips to the rubbish tip with the bundles of old newspapers.

We heard later that they had, out of curiosity, opened the (11) *last* / *least* / *latest* of

the bundles, (12) *it* / *which* / *they* contained newspapers dating from 1954, the

year when the twins (13) *were* / *had* / *got* born. It was only (14) *so* / *when* / *then* that they

discovered that between the leaves of (15) *each* / *all* / *a* newspaper their crazy old

aunt had carefully put a rare and beautiful print. There (16) *shall* / *must* / *need* have

been fifty in that bundle alone. The nephews took the bundle with

(17) *its* / *their* / *her* precious contents to a dealer. They realised too late that in

(18) *throwing* / *throw* / *to throw* away all those bundles of newspapers, they (19) *were* / *have* / *had*

probably thrown away several thousands of pounds (20) *so* / *as well.* / *too*

[Adapted from 'A Load of Rubbish', in 'Happy Days and other very short stories' by Jake Allsop, published by Penguin Books, 1998].

28 Make, do or have

A   Place the following words under the correct headings. There is an
example at the beginning (0).

a bank account	a barbecue	a bath/shower	~~the bed~~
business	a celebration	a complaint	a confession
damage	a driving lesson	fun of someone	a fuss
the garden	harm	an impression	a journey	a mistake
a noise	one's best	a phone call	a profit/loss
research	the shopping	someone a favour	a speech

Make	Do	Have
0 _the bed_	1 _____	1 _____
1 _____	2 _____	2 _____
2 _____	3 _____	3 _____
3 _____	4 _____	4 _____
4 _____	5 _____	5 _____
5 _____	6 _____	
6 _____	7 _____	
7 _____	8 _____	
8 _____		
9 _____		
10 _____		
11 _____		

B Now fill in the gaps in the following sentences with the correct form of *make*, *do* or *have*. There is an example at the beginning (0).

0 Why do politicians always take so long to _____*make*_____ decisions?

1 It's time you _____ a holiday, Margaret. It will _____ you the world of good.

2 Everyone over the age of thirty should _____ a will.

3 Your daughter is _____ excellent progress, Mrs Grove. She ought to _____ well in next year's exams.

4 It _____ no difference to me when you finish it, as long as you _____ a good job.

5 I've decided to _____ a big party on my birthday. Could I leave you to _____ the arrangements, darling?

6 You must _____ the exam, I'm afraid. You _____ no alternative.

7 The two countries _____ talks last week and are optimistic about _____ peace soon.

8 Take this medicine. It will _____ you good.

9 This photograph doesn't _____ Sally justice. She's much better-looking really.

10 If we are going to _____ this company profitable again we are going to have to _____ a lot of changes.

11 I must _____ an appointment to get my eyes tested.

12 Do you mind if I _____ a suggestion?

13 I _____ a really good time on holiday and
    _____ lots of friends.

14 I hope you don't think I'm _____ excuses, but I
    really must stay in tonight and _____ my hair.

15 'How's Sylvia getting on in America?'
    'Oh, she's _____ the time of her life. In fact, she's
    _____ plans to settle there.'

16 'You see your parents quite often. You must _____ a
    good relationship with them.'
    'No, not really. It's more a question of _____ one's
    duty.'

17 We moved closer together to _____ room for Annie
    to sit down.

18 Swedish cars _____ a very good reputation for
    quality and safety.

19 They _____ us a very good offer for our flat.

Make/do + noun expressions
Why do we say **make** *a mistake* but **do** *your homework*? *Make* has the idea
of creating (producing) something which didn't exist before; *do* has the idea
of performing an action on something which already exists. But does this
help you to understand why we say **make** *the bed* and **do** *business*? In the
end, it is easier just to memorise the whole expression! And if you are not
sure, use *make*.

Use of English Part 1
Cloze with multiple choice

In the examination ...

- Parts 1 and 2 in the Use of English paper consist of a text with gaps (missing words). In Part 1, you are offered four alternatives from which to choose the one that fits in the gap. Mostly all the alternatives fit grammatically, but only one makes sense. (A sentence such as *I like to wear an elephant on my head.* is grammatically correct, but it makes no sense). You need therefore to look carefully at the meaning of the whole sentence to see which word makes sense.

- Beware of false friends! Examiners love to test words like *control*, *pretend* and *actual*, because these words look like words in other languages, but mean something different.

'The policeman is trying to control the traffic.'

29 Cloze with multiple choice 1

Read the text below and decide which answer A, B, C or D best fits each space. There is an example at the beginning (0).

A LUCKY ESCAPE

This is about an extraordinary incident that took place in London a few years ago. It was a day (0) ___*B*___ any other. On one of the city's underground stations, a train was (1) _____ the platform. Suddenly, a young woman (2) _____ herself into the path of the moving train. The horrified driver slammed on the brakes, certain that there was no way to stop the train before the woman was (3) _____ under the wheels.

But miraculously the train did stop. The first carriage had to be jacked up to free the badly (4) _____ woman, but the wheels had not passed over her and she (5) _____ .

The young woman (6) _____ out to be a gifted architect who was recovering from a nervous (7) _____ . Her amazing rescue from death was based on a remarkable (8) _____ , for the subsequent (9) _____ into the accident revealed that the train had not stopped during the driver's hasty breaking. It was revealed that, seconds before, a passenger had (10) _____ down the emergency handle, which automatically (11) _____ the brakes of the train.

The passenger had had no particular reason for doing so, but had acted (12) _____ . Unbelievable as it sounds, he was completely (13) _____ of the fact that a young woman was about to hurl herself into the path of the oncoming train.

In fact, the Transport Authority (14) _____ prosecuting the passenger on the grounds that he had had no (15) _____ cause for using the emergency system!

0	**A** so	**B** like	**C** by	**D** such
1	**A** arriving	**B** approaching	**C** catching	**D** advancing
2	**A** leapt	**B** tossed	**C** plunged	**D** threw
3	**A** crushed	**B** smashed	**C** broken	**D** squeezed
4	**A** damaged	**B** wounded	**C** injured	**D** harmed
5	**A** succeeded	**B** overcame	**C** survived	**D** continued
6	**A** proved	**B** came	**C** made	**D** turned
7	**A** breakdown	**B** failure	**C** outbreak	**D** setback
8	**A** coincidence	**B** correspondence	**C** occasion	**D** opportunity
9	**A** examination	**B** inquiry	**C** view	**D** search
10	**A** taken	**B** handed	**C** pulled	**D** lifted
11	**A** joins	**B** applies	**C** presses	**D** attaches
12	**A** for a change	**B** by accident	**C** at random	**D** on impulse
13	**A** uninformed	**B** unsure	**C** unaware	**D** uncertain
14	**A** considered	**B** meant	**C** advised	**D** faced
15	**A** noticeable	**B** expected	**C** correct	**D** reasonable

30 Cloze with multiple choice 2

Read the text below and decide which answer A, B, C or D best fits each space. There is an example at the beginning (0).

HAPPINESS

In recent years there has been a remarkable increase in (0) ____A____ into happiness. The researchers have (1) _____ a number of factors which contribute to a definition of happiness.

First of all, there is, in some people, a moderate genetic predisposition to be happy: in other words, happiness (2) _____ in families. And happiness seems to correlate quite (3) _____ with the main dimensions of personality: extroverts are generally happier, neurotics are less so.

Second, people often (4) _____ good social relations as a reason for their happiness. In particular, friends are a great (5) _____ of joy, partly because of the agreeable things they do together, partly because of the way friends use positive non-verbal (6) _____ , such as caressing and touching, to affirm their friendship. Marriage and similar (7) _____ relationships can also form the basis of lasting happiness.

Third, job satisfaction undoubtedly (8) _____ overall satisfaction, and vice versa – perhaps this is why some people are happy in boring jobs: it (9) _____ both ways. Job satisfaction is caused not only by the essential nature of the work, but (10) _____ by social interactions with co-workers. Unemployment, on the (11) _____ , can be a serious cause of unhappiness.

Fourth, leisure is important because it is more under individual (12) _____ than most other causes of happiness. Activities (13) _____ sport and music, and participation in voluntary work and social clubs of various kinds, can give great joy. This is partly because of the (14) _____ themselves, but also because of the social support of other group members – it is very strong (15) _____ the case of religious groups.

0	A research	B inquiry	C examination	D study
1	A fallen back on	B gone in for	C got down to	D come up with
2	A arrives	B runs	C goes	D descends
3	A strongly	B nearly	C firmly	D hardly
4	A explain	B prefer	C talk	D report
5	A meaning	B origin	C base	D source
6	A movements	B motions	C slogans	D signals
7	A near	B close	C tight	D heavy
8	A consists of	B applies to	C contributes to	D counts on
9	A works	B effects	C makes	D turns
10	A too	B as well	C also	D plus
11	A common	B contrast	C comparison	D contrary
12	A check	B power	C control	D choice
13	A like	B such	C so	D thus
14	A facilities	B activities	C exercises	D amenities
15	A by	B for	C in	D with

31 Cloze with multiple choice 3

Read the text below and decide which answer A, B, C or D best fits each space. There is an example at the beginning (0).

A FAIR WAGE?

What constitutes a fair wage? The **(0)** ____*A*____ of money that people earn is **(1)** _____ determined not by fairness but by market forces. This fact, however, should not **(2)** _____ us trying to devise a mechanism for deciding what is the right pay for the job.

A **(3)** _____ point for such an investigation would be to try to decide the ratio which ought to **(4)** _____ between the highest and the lowest paid. The picture **(5)** _____ more complicated by two factors. The first is the 'social wage', that is, the benefits – **(6)** _____ as holidays, sick pay and maternity leave – which every citizen is **(7)** _____ to.

Secondly, the taxation system is often used as an **(8)** _____ of social justice by taxing the rich at a very high **(9)** _____ indeed.

Allowing for these two things, most countries now **(10)** _____ as socially acceptable a ratio of 7:1 between the best and the **(11)** _____ paid.

If the ratio is narrower, the highly-qualified people who usually **(12)** _____ heavy responsibilities may become so dissatisfied that they **(13)** _____ emigrating (the so-called 'brain drain').

But, if it is wider, the **(14)** _____ between rich and poor will be so great that it will **(15)** _____ to social tension and, in extreme cases, to violence and revolution.

0	**A** amount	**B** size	**C** lot	**D** sum
1	**A** by all means	**B** for instance	**C** in reality	**D** out of the question
2	**A** admit	**B** prevent	**C** forbid	**D** prohibit
3	**A** opening	**B** beginning	**C** starting	**D** commencing
4	**A** remain	**B** exist	**C** stand	**D** become
5	**A** results	**B** is drawn	**C** becomes	**D** is made
6	**A** such	**B** so	**C** just	**D** like
7	**A** ensured	**B** enabled	**C** entrusted	**D** entitled
8	**A** engine	**B** instrument	**C** appliance	**D** apparatus
9	**A** rate	**B** cost	**C** range	**D** value
10	**A** require	**B** regard	**C** review	**D** respect
11	**A** smallest	**B** least	**C** lowest	**D** fewest
12	**A** hold	**B** wear	**C** carry	**D** bring
13	**A** pull away	**B** turn out	**C** set off	**D** end up
14	**A** gap	**B** space	**C** hole	**D** size
15	**A** drive	**B** lead	**C** aim	**D** urge

32 Cloze with multiple choice 4

Read the text below and decide which answer A, B, C or D best fits each space. There is an example at the beginning (0).

DO-IT-YOURSELF COMPUTERS

Building (0) _____A_____ own computer may appear a difficult task. But if you have had one (1) _____ and have even progressed to being able to, say, (2) _____ a video card, you are ready to enter the do-it-yourself PC business.

In choosing the components, even something as basic as the case can (3) _____ a difference.

(4) _____ the computer magazines and you will see that cases come in all sort of shapes and sizes: small, tall, wide, narrow – whatever you (5) _____ .

If you think you would like to have ten hard disks in your computer, you can find a case to (6) _____ your needs. If you want a case that will (7) _____ in a drawer, that is available too. You can (8) _____ your requirements and get exactly the machine you want: everything, from the sound card and graphics cards to the backup device of your (9) _____ .

Of course, (10) _____ or later, something will go wrong. If you get (11) _____ crashes, is it the memory chip, the CPU, the hard disk or the software that is (12) _____ ? You could (13) _____ yourself having to deal with all the various manufacturers of the different pieces in order to find out (14) _____ piece or program is causing the problem.

So, if you want to become a DIY expert, start by upgrading your existing machine, and you may soon have the (15) _____ you need to continue.

0	A your	B an	C the	D its
1	A in time	B for a while	C at the moment	D since then
2	A put	B install	C place	D set
3	A make	B do	C give	D take
4	A Revise	B Control	C Check	D Inspect
5	A dream	B fancy	C hope	D long
6	A respond	B call	C fill	D meet
7	A arrange	B conform	C fit	D get
8	A satisfy	B notify	C qualify	D specify
9	A choice	B pick	C selection	D pleasing
10	A before	B sooner	C earlier	D after
11	A occasional	B seldom	C rare	D sometimes
12	A in trouble	B by mistake	C out of use	D at fault
13	A get	B leave	C find	D stop
14	A their	B who's	C the	D whose
15	A trust	B confidence	C belief	D wish

33 Cloze with multiple choice 5

Read the text below and decide which answer A, B, C or D best fits each space. There is an example at the beginning (0).

THE NEW CHINA

All is not well in the state of China. Most people who **(0)** ___*A*___ an interest in China know that, in the days when all industry was **(1)** _____ by the state, the workers had their basic needs taken care of. They did not **(2)** _____ much, but they could be sure of a house or flat, health care, education and a pension.

This was the 'iron rice-bowl'. But what happens when the bowl breaks, as is happening now with the **(3)** _____ of private industry and the end of the welfare state?

The trend is clear. In some provinces, fewer than half the workers are now **(4)** _____ by the state. By the end of the next decade, at least a quarter of China's **(5)** _____ will be privately or self employed. When this happens, China will need to look for ways of replacing state welfare.

Take housing. Foreign companies increasingly **(6)** _____ housing in order to attract the workers they want. As to health care, the end of free medicine is already **(7)** _____ . Under the old system, if a state worker needed **(8)** _____ , the hospital simply sent the bill to his factory. Today, state firms **(9)** _____ part of the fee from a worker's pay.

Some even **(10)** _____ private medical insurance. **(11)** _____ pensions are concerned, personal pensions, bought through life insurance companies, are said to be growing in number by 25% a year. Many towns are experimenting with pooled pension funds from all businesses, state and private, with workers **(12)** _____ about two percent of their income. This **(13)** _____ well in places with lots of young people and high growth, but in areas of declining economy, pooling means more people getting less.

Taken with China's other problems – **(14)** _____ inflation, rising unemployment and an increasing crime rate in the big cities – it is not surprising that some people **(15)** _____ the coming of private enterprise as a mixed blessing.

0	A take	B make	C play	D bring
1	A run	B held	C ruled	D governed
2	A spend	B gain	C earn	D pay
3	A growth	B inflation	C outburst	D addition
4	A overtaken	B used	C requested	D employed
5	A staff	B workforce	C personnel	D manpower
6	A propose	B offer	C invite	D suggest
7	A at present	B on time	C in sight	D under suspicion
8	A health	B cure	C remedy	D treatment
9	A deduct	B reduce	C expect	D discharge
10	A speak for	B insist on	C hold with	D take in
11	A Although	B As long as	C Also	D As far as
12	A combining	B withdrawing	C contributing	D receiving
13	A works	B makes	C does	D comes
14	A wide	B high	C fast	D big
15	A regret	B recall	C regard	D respect

34 Cloze with multiple choice 6

Read the text below and decide which answer A, B, C or D best fits each space. There is an example at the beginning (0).

FAMILY TREE

What do you know about the (0) ____*A*____ of your family? Tracing your ancestors can be a very interesting (1) _____ . But, if you don't go (2) _____ it in a methodical (3) _____ , it can also become very frustrating. If you want to (4) _____ progress with your 'family tree' without tearing your hair out in frustration, there are some simple rules which you should (5) _____ .

First of all, note the names of your (6) _____ family and draw a rough family tree, starting with yourself at the bottom. Don't worry if you can only go back as (7) _____ as your grandparents.

You will have made a good start, especially if you can fill (8) _____ most of the dates relating to births, marriages and deaths (BM&D for (9) _____).

Next, write down the names of all older (10) _____ who are still alive: grandfathers, grandmothers, great-aunts and great-uncles can be a mine of information.

You often find that they have originals of BM&D certificates, in which (11) _____ , ask nicely for copies because this will (12) _____ you time and money. They might also have family Bibles (13) _____ information going back many years, or photo (14) _____ and other documents that will help you in your search.

Thirdly, look in telephone directories for other possible family contacts. This is particularly valuable if you have a really (15) _____ surname. Of course, if your name is a common one such as Smith or Brown, this is less (16) _____ to be worthwhile, (17) _____ you know that yours is a local family, or one which has stayed in the same business for (18) _____ generations.

After that, you will be ready to visit places that keep official
(19) _____ : libraries, registry offices and so on. But
(20) _____ that until after you have done all the groundwork.
Have fun!

0	**A** history	**B** legend	**C** story	**D** report
1	**A** leisure	**B** game	**C** sport	**D** hobby
2	**A** to	**B** for	**C** after	**D** about
3	**A** route	**B** way	**C** work	**D** task
4	**A** do	**B** have	**C** make	**D** take
5	**A** correspond	**B** succeed	**C** follow	**D** answer
6	**A** immediate	**B** next	**C** actual	**D** recent
7	**A** long	**B** far	**C** near	**D** soon
8	**A** off	**B** up	**C** out	**D** in
9	**A** short	**B** letters	**C** brief	**D** initials
10	**A** parents	**B** cousins	**C** relatives	**D** families
11	**A** matter	**B** fall	**C** way	**D** case
12	**A** spare	**B** save	**C** keep	**D** prevent
13	**A** receiving	**B** containing	**C** enclosing	**D** presenting
14	**A** files	**B** books	**C** catalogues	**D** albums
15	**A** unheard	**B** unknown	**C** unusual	**D** unwanted
16	**A** possible	**B** useful	**C** likely	**D** interesting
17	**A** unless	**B** although	**C** except	**D** in case
18	**A** several	**B** more	**C** long	**D** few
19	**A** volumes	**B** records	**C** accounts	**D** works
20	**A** let	**B** resist	**C** stop	**D** leave

Use of English Part 2
Cloze with gaps

In the examination ...

In this part, there are gaps but no alternatives are given. You have to find a word that (a) fits grammatically (b) makes sense. In making your choice of the word to go in the gap, check first that it makes sense; and secondly that it is grammatically correct.

Note that, although the examiners try to make sure that there is only one possibility, there may sometimes be more than one solution.

Many of the words tested are 'structural' words like auxiliary verbs, modals, articles and prepositions.

This is also the place where 'collocations' are tested, that is, fixed expressions such as *make fun of, fall in love with, by means of, look down on.*

'Falling in love'

35 Cloze with gaps 1

Read the text below and think of the word which best fits each space. Use only one word in each space. There is an example at the beginning (0).

THE NEW PET

Harry Dawson's two children, Mark and Sarah, were overjoyed
(0) ___when___ he came home one day with a scruffy black and
white mongrel (1) _____ the local Dog's Home. The children
(2) _____ to call it 'Lucky'.

A few days (3) _____ , Harry Dawson felt less happy
(4) _____ the new family pet when Lucky came
(5) _____ the kitchen with a dead rabbit in (6) _____
mouth.

The creature was quite fat and (7) _____ -groomed and was
obviously a pet (8) _____ than a wild rabbit.

Sarah (9) _____ one look at the rabbit and immediately
identified it as (10) _____ to her friend, Cathy Blake, who lived
next door (11) _____ one.

Fortunately, the Blake family were away (12) _____ holiday in
the south of France. So (13) _____ dark that evening, Harry
Dawson sneaked into the Blakes' garden. After making
(14) _____ that he was not (15) _____ watched, he took
the dead rabbit out of the plastic bag in which he (16) _____
been carrying it, and put it (17) _____ the empty hutch*.

There were (18) _____ teeth marks at all on the rabbit, so he
was sure that the Blakes (19) _____ assume it had died of
natural causes.

By the (20) _____ the Blakes returned from their holiday, the
Dawsons had more or (21) _____ forgotten the incident. Then,
Harry Dawson happened to bump (22) _____ Mr Blake in the
post office. Politely, he asked him (23) _____ his family was.

'They're very well, thank you,' said Mr Blake. 'But my daughter, Cathy, is very **(24)** _____ .'

'Oh, sorry to hear that! She's **(25)** _____ a happy child as a rule. What happened to **(26)** _____ her feel that way?'

Mr Blake shook **(27)** _____ head as he went **(28)** _____ :

'Her pet rabbit died the week before we left for France, and **(29)** _____ really sick person **(30)** _____ gone and put a dead rabbit in its cage!'

(*a cage for rabbits and other pets, usually made of wood)

36 Cloze with gaps 2

Read the text below and think of the word which best fits each space. Use only one word in each space. There is an example at the beginning (0).

EXPERTS

My friend Miguel knows an incredible amount **(0)** ___*about*___ football. He can recite the names of **(1)** _____ the players. He can **(2)** _____ you the result of every match and **(3)** _____ scored the goals. He knows the history of **(4)** _____ football club you care to name.

Moreover, he is **(5)** _____ knowledgeable about Italian or German or Brazilian football as he is about the football of **(6)** _____ own country. Thanks **(7)** _____ a photographic memory, he has acquired an encyclopaedic knowledge of the game.

He **(8)** _____ a lot of time looking through the sports sections of the newspapers, from which he **(9)** _____ the information he needs in **(10)** _____ to make endless lists and carry **(11)** _____ statistical calculations of all kinds.

(12) _____ short, he is an expert, although, curiously **(13)** _____ , he does not play the game **(14)** _____ , and only goes occasionally to **(15)** _____ a match.

I admire Miguel **(16)** _____ his expertise, but I have to admit that he **(17)** _____ me feel inadequate. I want to be an expert on something too, **(18)** _____ doesn't really matter what, as **(19)** _____ as I can find a subject about **(20)** _____ I know more than anyone **(21)** _____ .

It is said **(22)** _____ , in studying any subject, you go through four stages:

At **(23)** _____ , you know nothing and you *know* that you don't know **(24)** _____ .

Stage Two: you know a little and you think you know a lot.

By the (25) _____ you reach Stage Three, you know a lot but you think you know very little.

When you get to Stage Four, you (26) _____ arrived: you know a lot and you *know* that you know a lot.

(27) _____ my friend Miguel, I never seem to get beyond Stage One. Wait a minute, though! There is one subject I am good at: natural history. I mean, I (28) _____ name every bird, animal and plant I (29) _____ across on an afternoon's walk. I know a *lot* – or do I? Perhaps I am only at Stage Two after (30) _____ .

37 Cloze with gaps 3

Read the text below and think of the word which best fits each space. Use only one word in each space. There is an example at the beginning (0).

JAVANESE NEW MOON

It was the night of the full moon, an event **(0)** _which/that_ always drives Java's young people **(1)** _____ with excitement.

Fireworks were lit long **(2)** _____ the moon came **(3)** _____ . The noise of firecrackers brought people out **(4)** _____ the warm night to enjoy the spectacle. Everywhere, there were the paper **(5)** _____ of used fireworks lying **(6)** _____ the ground. Little boys lit more and covered **(7)** _____ ears as they **(8)** _____ excitedly for the explosions.

The moon appeared above the horizon: a huge, silver ball **(9)** _____ above the city, and the streets **(10)** _____ with people, as Java began to enjoy **(11)** _____ of the year's greatest events: 'the Night of the Full Moon', a festival **(12)** _____ is especially popular **(13)** _____ young people.

More and **(14)** _____ young Javanese gathered **(15)** _____ and walked slowly through the dark night. Joking and chatting, they moved towards the mountain **(16)** _____ the edge of the city. They continued to climb **(17)** _____ they reached the ancient temple at the **(18)** _____ of the mountain.

(19) _____ they were inside the temple, they drank their water and **(20)** _____ their 'mooncakes' – delicious home-**(21)** _____ cookies, full of dried fruit and nuts. Outside, on the mountain, teenagers sat cross-legged **(22)** _____ circles, chatting and telling each **(23)** _____ jokes. And still, in **(24)** _____ hundreds, more young people continued to make their **(25)** _____ up the mountain to stare **(26)** _____ the brightly shining moon.

By midnight, the fireworks **(27)** _____ stopped whizzing up from the grey city in the valley **(28)** _____ them. But **(29)** _____ the night, the sound of firecrackers continued to **(30)** _____ heard from the suburbs.

38 Cloze with gaps 4

Read the text below and think of the word which best fits each space. Use only one word in each space. There is an example at the beginning (0).

CALL ME MOTHER

It was **(0)** ___*their*___ first wedding anniversary and to celebrate it Colin and his wife, Julie, decided to go **(1)** _____ a meal at one of the **(2)** _____ expensive restaurants in town. They were **(3)** _____ a romantic evening, gazing lovingly **(4)** _____ each other's eyes, when they noticed an elderly lady sitting alone **(5)** _____ in their direction.

They smiled back politely and a few minutes **(6)** _____ the old lady **(7)** _____ her way to their table.

'I'm terrible sorry to **(8)** _____ you,' she said, wiping away a tear. 'But you look just **(9)** _____ my son. He was killed in a car accident just over a year ago and I **(10)** _____ miss him terribly. I wonder if you'd **(11)** _____ me a favour?'

The couple were very moved by the old lady and, feeling sorry **(12)** _____ her, agreed to help **(13)** _____ they could.

'I wonder if, just as I'm leaving, you **(14)** _____ say 'Goodbye, Mum' and wave me off? It would give me **(15)** _____ a thrill.'

'Of **(16)** _____ we will!' the couple replied. 'No problem!'

Well, **(17)** _____ could they possibly refuse?

The old lady thanked them and went **(18)** _____ to her table. **(19)** _____ a short while, she picked up all her belongings and got up to leave.

'Goodbye, Mum!' shouted the couple with a big, theatrical wave as the old lady **(20)** _____ her way slowly out **(21)** _____ the restaurant.

'See you at the weekend,' Colin added.

They had (22) _____ their 'good deed for the day', and were feeling very pleased with (23) _____ .

'(24) _____ a dear old lady!' said Julie. She smiled (25) _____ Colin. 'That was a nice thing you (26) _____ for her, darling!'

They finished their meal and asked for the (27) _____ . But after checking and rechecking it, they sent (28) _____ the manager, demanding to know (29) _____ they had been overcharged by more than forty pounds.

'But the total amount (30) _____ the cost of three meals: yours, your wife's and your mother's,' the manager explained.

'What?' the man exclaimed.

'Yes, your mother said "My son will pay"!'

39 Cloze with gaps 5

Read the text below and think of the word which best fits each space. Use only one word in each space. There is an example at the beginning (0).

ANNA MIKOVA

Sculpture, as a fine art in Ruthelia, dates (0) ___*back*___ only to the 1920s. (1) _____ of Ruthelia's first sculptors was a woman called Anna Mikova.

Anna (2) _____ born in Azhgorod in 1904, and as a child (3) _____ the local elementary school. When her father (4) _____ a job in Damascus, she continued her education there. Then, her family returned to Ruthelia and settled (5) _____ the island of Belikstrana, where Anna completed her secondary education. Her love of art (6) _____ always evident in the pictures she drew at school and at home. In 1920, before graduating (7) _____ high school, she began to attend (8) _____ in painting at the Academy of Fine Arts. There she made a copy of an ancient bust, and (9) _____ her teacher saw it, he could not at (10) _____ believe that it was Anna's own work.

(11) _____ studying painting for a year, she chose to study sculpture. She was the first and the only female student (12) _____ three boys at the Academy. She (13) _____ first in a competition, (14) _____ a scholarship and went to Italy. She attended the studio of Professor Luppi at the Rome Academy of Fine Arts, and (15) _____ was there that her work gained maturity. She later became assistant to Edolo di Girolamo, the Italian sculptor (16) _____ designed the Gloria Monument in Zorica Square in Azhgorod.

Her passion for sculpture was (17) _____ strong that she earned a reputation (18) _____ as well as in Ruthelia. She was a productive artist whose work (19) _____ in many exhibitions. Her sculptures, (20) _____ as her statues of the President and his wife, attracted widespread interest.

She (21) _____ to work throughout her life. Her husband, Sergei Mikov retired, (22) _____ served as an ambassador for many years, and the couple moved back to the capital. After her husband's death and the marriage (23) _____ her adopted daughter, Anna went (24) _____ producing sculptures. (25) _____ is generally agreed that this was her best period, when she produced some of her finest work, (26) _____ the famous 'Hymn to Life' series of sculptures.

She died on 2 October 1992 (27) _____ skin cancer. It was said that at her funeral (28) _____ were more than ten thousand mourners, and (29) _____ one of them was (30) _____ tears.

40 Cloze with gaps 6

Read the text below and think of the word which best fits each space. Use only one word in each space. There is an example at the beginning (0).

THE HITCH-HIKER

It was a very wet day. In fact, it had (0) ___*been*___ pouring down the (1) _____ morning, and David Williams was (2) _____ to the skin (3) _____ he stood at the side of the road (4) _____ to hitch a lift. (5) _____ far, only four cars had (6) _____ along, and each one had gone past (7) _____ stopping. David was beginning to wonder if anyone (8) _____ stop for him when a truck suddenly (9) _____ up. The driver wound down his window, looked at David's soaking wet clothes, and immediately (10) _____ pity on him.

As there was (11) _____ room in the cab, he told David to hop on the back. David accepted (12) _____ thanks and quickly climbed aboard. In the back (13) _____ was an empty coffin. (14) _____ it was still raining heavily, David decided to climb (15) _____ it for shelter. Standing by the roadside had (16) _____ him feel very tired, so it wasn't (17) _____ before he had fallen fast asleep.

While he was sleeping, the truck (18) _____ stopped again to (19) _____ up another hitch-hiker. Like David, he too climbed on to the back of the truck. (20) _____ this time, it had (21) _____ raining and the sun had come (22) _____ . It began to (23) _____ very hot inside the coffin and David suddenly woke up. Without thinking, he lifted the lid (24) _____ the coffin, saw the stranger standing there and shouted: 'Wow, I (25) _____ have fallen asleep!'

His fellow hitch-hiker took one (26) _____ at David, screamed (27) _____ fear and jumped off the truck. Needless to say, he has never hitchhiked (28) _____ that day!

Use of English Part 3 Sentence transformation

In the examination ....

There are certain kinds of transformations that the examiners are very fond of:

- active to passive

  Newton discovered gravity. → Gravity was discovered by Newton.

- conditionals

  I was ill so I couldn't go. → If I hadn't been so ill, I could have gone.

- comparatives

  John is taller than Jane. → Jane isn't as/so tall as John.

- reported speech

  'Go away!' he said → He told us to go away

- related words

  How much did you pay for it? → How much did it cost you?

- related expressions

  It was so hot that ... → It was such a hot day that ...

- tense 'traps'

  I haven't seen her for a long time. → It's a long time since I last saw her.

  I shouldn't have done it. → I wish I hadn't done it.

- collocations

  I spent twenty minutes on that puzzle. → It took me twenty minutes to do that puzzle.

'He spent twenty minutes on that puzzle.'

41 Sentence transformation 1

Complete the second sentence so that it has a similar meaning to the first sentence, using the word given. **Do not change the word given.** You must use between two and five words, including the word given. There is an example at the beginning (0).

0 This hotel is full.

vacancies

There _____ *are no vacancies at* _____ this hotel.

1 We were surprised to see Katie at the party.

expect

We _____ to see Katie at the party.

2 Everyone has heard about the canals in Amsterdam.

famous

Amsterdam _____ canals.

3 Our driving laws and theirs are not the same.

different

Our driving laws _____ theirs.

4 Is this pen yours?

belong

Does _____ you?

5 Why wouldn't she give you her telephone number?

refuse

Why _____ you her telephone number?

6 How much did that jacket cost?

pay

How much _____ that jacket?

7 Is it necessary for me to confirm my reservation ?

need

Do _____ confirm my reservation?

8 I completed that jigsaw puzzle in twenty minutes.

took

It _____ complete that jigsaw puzzle.

9 Smoking in the library is against the rules.

allowed

You _____ in the library.

10 It was such a stale cake that nobody wanted to eat it.

so

The cake _____ that nobody wanted to eat it.

42 Sentence transformation 2

Complete the second sentence so that it has a similar meaning to the first sentence, using the word given. **Do not change the word given**. You must use between two and five words, including the word given. There is an example at the beginning (0).

0 The tea was so hot that we couldn't drink it.

too

The tea was _____*too hot for us to*_____ drink.

1 She needs less sleep than I do.

more

I need _____ she does.

2 It was such a horrifying film that I could not sleep.

so

The film _____ that I could not sleep.

3 Is it necessary for me to come with you?

have

Do _____ come with you?

4 She didn't say goodbye when she left.

without

She _____ goodbye.

5 'I'm sorry I'm late,' he said.

apologized

He _____ late.

6 I don't have much money so I can't go on holiday.

could

If I _____ go on holiday.

7 I don't really want to go out tonight.

prefer

I _____ go out tonight.

8 My uncle had never been abroad before.

trip

It was _____ abroad.

9 It will be wonderful to see you in the summer.

forward

I am _____ you in the summer.

10 We worked on the computer all morning.

spent

We _____ on the computer.

43 Sentence transformation 3

Complete the second sentence so that it has a similar meaning to the first sentence, using the word given. **Do not change the word given.** You must use between two and five words, including the word given. There is an example at the beginning (0).

0 She's very excited about going on holiday.

looking

She's ___*looking forward to going*___ on holiday.

1 It was the first time I had ever seen a bullfight.

never

I _____ a bullfight before.

2 Their wedding takes place on Saturday.

married

They _____ on Saturday.

3 Sarah is one of our most hard working secretaries.

harder

None of our secretaries _____ Sarah.

4 John won first prize in the competition.

awarded

John _____ first prize in the competition.

5 Jimmy works harder than Kevin.

as

Kevin doesn't _____ Jimmy.

6 The party was so boring that I left early.

such

It _____ that I left early.

7 Can you do the shopping tomorrow?

able

Will _____ the shopping tomorrow?

8 The Dean has sent a special report to the Rector.

been

The Rector _____ a special report by the Dean.

9 Mozart was thirty-five when he died.

age

Mozart _____ thirty-five.

10 'Will you lend me five pounds?' he asked.

borrow

He asked if _____ five pounds.

44 Sentence transformation 4

Complete the second sentence so that it has a similar meaning to the first sentence, using the word given. **Do not change the word given.** You must use between two and five words, including the word given. There is an example at the beginning (0).

0 Paul likes music.

interested

Paul _____ *is interested in* _____ music.

1 I certainly won't go there again!

last

That _____ I go there!

2 It was really very bad of you to steal the Crown Jewels.

should

You _____ the Crown Jewels.

3 I have never travelled by plane before.

first

This is _____ travelled by plane.

4 I didn't go shopping so I couldn't buy you that sweater.

bought

If I had gone shopping, _____ you that sweater.

5 Detectives have been investigating the murder for two months.

started

It's two months _____ investigating the murder.

6 'I'm sorry, I didn't give details of the meeting,' said Paul.

apologized

Paul _____ details of the meeting.

7 'Don't overwater the plants!' my mother said.

told

My mother _____ overwater the plants.

8 I regret not going to university.

wish

I _____ to university.

9 He found it really hard to start the car.

difficulty

He _____ the car.

10 John and I quarrelled over a week ago.

out

John and I _____ a week ago.

45 Sentence transformation 5

Complete the second sentence so that it has a similar meaning to the first sentence, using the word given. **Do not change the word given**. You must use between two and five words, including the word given. There is an example at the beginning (0).

0 'What's the date today?' Michael asked.

know

Michael ___*wanted to know what*___ the date was today.

1 David was too ill to go camping with us.

enough

David _____ to go camping with us.

2 'Will you take the dog for a walk?'

asked

He _____ the dog for a walk.

3 This is the best food I've ever eaten.

better

I've _____ this.

4 It's ages since I last saw John.

seen

I _____ for ages.

5 Our teacher doesn't speak loudly enough for us to hear.

quietly

Our teacher speaks _____ for us to hear.

6 We didn't go out because it was raining.

had

If _____ , we would have gone out.

7 I should very much like to be able to play the guitar.

wish

I _____ play the guitar.

8 The pop star avoided the press by leaving by a side door.

order

The pop star left by a side door _____ the press.

9 He was punished for his bad behaviour.

badly

If he _____ , he would not have been punished.

10 I have never been in a submarine before.

time

This is _____ been in a submarine.

46 Sentence transformation 6

Complete the second sentence so that it has a similar meaning to the first sentence, using the word given. **Do not change the word given.** You must use between two and five words, including the word given. There is an example at the beginning (0).

0 Is she Australian?

come

Does _____ *she come from* _____ Australia?

1 The only question I had wrong was question seven.

except

I had _____ question seven.

2 Don't go if you don't feel like it.

point

There's _____ if you don't feel like it.

3 They continued to play despite the heavy rain.

though

They continued to play, even _____ .

4 After nearly an hour the coach had still not arrived.

sign

After nearly an hour _____ of the coach.

5 How likely is she to win the race?

chances

What are _____ the race?

6 If you pay no attention to him, he'll soon go away.

notice

If you _____ him, he'll soon go away.

7 I don't really want you to set fire to the Town Hall.

rather

I _____ set fire to the Town Hall.

8 Sally hasn't contacted us for over six weeks.

heard

We _____ over six weeks ago.

9 'You really must stay the night,' he said to us.

insisted

He _____ the night.

10 It is a pity I saw that confidential letter.

seen

I wish _____ that confidential letter.

Use of English Part 4
Error correction

In the examination ...

The errors are usually the 'little words' like prepositions, verbs and adverbs. The examiners have one or two favourite tricks, especially mixing up two expressions by adding a word which belongs to the word before it, but not to the word after it.

A few examples:

- *After finishing my degree, I took **out** a job in a big computer company.*
  Here, the confusion is between the verb *take out* and the expression *take a job*.

- *I will have no **any** difficulty.*
  Here the confusion is between *have no difficulty* and *not have any difficulty*, made even more confusing by the possibility of *not any difficulty* (although not in this context).

- *My teacher will be **too** pleased to support my application.*
  Here the confusion is between *My teacher will be pleased to ...* and *My teacher will be only too pleased to ...*

The only way to beat the examiner is by very careful reading of ALL the words, especially the 'little words'.

'After finishing his degree, he took a job in a big computer company.'

47 Error correction 1

Read the text below and look carefully at each line. Some of the lines are correct, and some have a word which should not be there. If a line is correct put a tick (✓) after it. If a line has a word which should not be there, write the word after it. There are two examples at the beginning (0 and 00).

A GLASS OF ORANGE JUICE

0	The train was crowded and I as couldn't find anywhere to	_as_
00	sit. So, after searching every compartment for an empty	_✓_
1	seat without the success, I decided to pop along to	_____
2	the refreshment car, where you can usually get something up to	_____
3	drink and a bite to eat with. Even here, all the seats were taken,	_____
4	so I just had to stand at the bar. The only other person was	_____
5	standing at the bar was a strange-looking man wearing an	_____
6	enormous overcoat. This struck at me as very peculiar,	_____
7	because that it was a very hot day. He appeared to be drinking	_____
8	a glass of orange juice, but the funny thing about was that he	_____
9	kept both his hands tightly round the glass as if he was being	_____
10	afraid that someone might want steal it. After a while, he went	_____
11	out, presumably for to go to the toilet, but before leaving,	_____
12	he scribbled something on a piece of paper and left it	_____
13	beside the glass, in which was still half full.	_____
14	The note said: 'Do you not drink my orange juice, I have	_____
15	dipped my fingers in it.' Smiling to myself, I picked up	_____
16	the note, wrote it underneath 'So have I', and slipped quietly away.	_____

48 Error correction 2

Read the text below and look carefully at each line. Some of the lines are correct, and some have a word which should not be there. If a line is correct put a tick (✓) after it. If a line has a word which should not be there, write the word after it. There are two examples at the beginning (0 and 00).

A MEAL TO REMEMBER

0	A German couple who went to abroad	_to_
00	for a holiday have returned without their pet	✓
1	poodle, Greta, following after a very traumatic	_____
2	experience in a restaurant there.	_____
3	They were out dining one evening and, as so	_____
4	usual, had their pet poodle with them. Just	_____
5	after when they had ordered their meal, the dog	_____
6	started to whine, so that they asked a waiter	_____
7	come over to their table and pointed to the	_____
8	poodle while they made an eating motions to	_____
9	show they wanted it to be fed.	_____
10	Eventually as the waiter appeared to understand	_____
11	and took Greta off into the kitchen. About after	_____
12	an hour later, he came back with their main dish	_____
13	and when they picked up inside the silver lid they	_____
14	found out their poodle roasted inside, garnished	_____
15	with pepper, sauce and vegetables. The	_____
16	couple, suffering from emotional shock, have	_____
17	decided for to return to Hamburg immediately.	_____

SECTION 8

49 Error correction 3

Read the text below and look carefully at each line. Some of the lines are correct, and some have a word which should not be there. If a line is correct put a tick (✓) after it. If a line has a word which should not be there, write the word after it. There are two examples at the beginning (0 and 00).

A THANK YOU LETTER

Dear Chris,

0	I am writing to thank you for the	✓
00	wonderful birthday present you sent for me.	*for*
1	It was just what I wanted! Molly she says	
2	you shouldn't have spent so much of money	
3	but, like me, she really likes the painting.	
4	It will looks very nice above the fireplace.	
5	The birthday party it went off quite well.	
6	There were about fifteen of us altogether	
7	that including my parents and Molly's dad.	
8	We eventually got to the bed at about 2 o'clock	
9	in the morning! We were really tired!	
10	When are we going to see you, Alice and the kids	
11	again? It's been over a year now since then you	
12	were last here. Why don't you try come down for	
13	the weekend soon? You know everyone would love	
14	for to see you again and I know you and I will	
15	not have lots and lots to talk about!	
16	Write soon and I look very forward to seeing you	

again.
With best wishes,
Alan

50 Error correction 4

Read the text below and look carefully at each line. Some of the lines are correct, and some have a word which should not be there. If a line is correct put a tick (✓) after it. If a line has a word which should not be there, write the word after it. There are two examples at the beginning (0 and 00).

AN EMBARRASSING MOMENT

0	One of my most embarrassing moments happened	✓
00	when ever I went for an interview for a job as receptionist	ever
1	in a large hotel in Brighton. I had driven it there and, because	_____
2	of the traffic and the difficulty of finding the hotel, I was slightly	_____
3	late. I had just reached for the hotel car park, and was about	_____
4	to reverse into a parking space when a man in a big, white	_____
5	Mercedes drove into it. This is made me really angry so	_____
6	I wound down the window and swore at him, but as he just	_____
7	ignored me and walked away, to which made me even madder.	_____
8	To make matters worse, the car park was full, so far I had to wait	_____
9	another ten minutes before then I found an empty parking space.	_____
10	By this time, I was over a quarter of an hour late for the interview,	_____
11	so I have rushed to the manager's office, knocked on the door	_____
12	and walked in. When the manager looked me up, I nearly died:	_____
13	it was the same man that I had sworn at in the car park – he the	_____
14	one who had taken off my parking space. Happily, we both saw	_____
15	the funny side of things and if I got the job, but on one condition:	_____
16	that I promised never to swear at the guests!	_____

51 Error correction 5

Read the text below and look carefully at each line. Some of the lines are correct, and some have a word which should not be there. If a line is correct put a tick (✓) after it. If a line has a word which should not be there, write the word after it. There are two examples at the beginning (0 and 00).

THE LADY VANISHES

0	In 1889, an Englishwoman and her daughter, on a visit	✓
00	to the Great Exhibition in Paris, checked up into one of the	*up*
1	most expensive hotels there. Each they had her own room. The	_____
2	daughter wanted to have take in the sights and sounds of the	_____
3	city immediately but her mother, tired after the trip, wanted to	_____
4	sleep. The girl accordingly she went out alone, strolled the	_____
5	Champs Elysées and saw the Eiffel Tower. When has she	_____
6	returned to her mother's room for six hours later, she found it	_____
7	empty. There was no sign of her mother ever having been there.	_____
8	When she asked the manager he insisted on that no one at the	_____
9	hotel had seen her or her mother to check in. The mother had	_____
10	disappeared away! The desperate girl searched for weeks	_____
11	before that finally returning to England. She died ten years later	_____
12	in a mental hospital. So that what was the explanation? After the	_____
13	daughter had been gone sightseeing, her mother had complained	_____
14	to the hotel doctor that she felt ill. It turned out so that she	_____
15	had contracted the plague! Hotel staff were instructed but not to	_____
16	say a word to anyone about it, in case visitors panicked and left	
	the city. No one knows what happened to the mother.	_____

52 Error correction 6

Read the text below and look carefully at each line. Some of the lines are correct, and some have a word which should not be there. If a line is correct put a tick (✓) after it. If a line has a word which should not be there, write the word after it. There are two examples at the beginning (0 and 00).

THE THREE-LEGGED CHICKEN

0	A man was travelling on the freeway at about 70 miles an hour	✓
00	when he was overtaken by a chicken running at the speed in	the
1	the fast lane. It was a huge bird like, about the size of a camel, and it	
2	was doing at least a hundred ones! The most amazing thing about it	
3	was that it had three legs. The man increased in his speed to try to	
4	catch up with the three-legged chicken, but the bird ran more faster	
5	than ever. Finally, it left the freeway, went through a farmyard and	
6	disappeared across a field. The motorist, who had been followed	
7	the chicken, stopped his car, got out of and went over to speak to a	
8	farmer, who had also watched the chicken to run through his farm,	
9	across the field and out of the sight. The motorist listened in amazement	
10	as the farmer explained that he bred these giant chickens.	
11	'But why do you want me to breed chickens with three legs?'	
12	asked the bewildered motorist. 'Oh, it's very simple. I am really prefer	
13	chicken leg, my wife likes the leg best too, and my son also prefers	
14	chicken leg, so it seemed the easiest way for to satisfy all three of	
15	us.' The motorist thought about for a moment. 'I see. So, tell me	
16	something. What do they taste like?' 'I don't know it,' the farmer replied	
	sadly, 'We've never managed to catch one yet!'	

Use of English Part 5
World building

In the examination ...

This part of the Use of English paper tests your knowledge of affixes, the means by which words are changed into other related words. There are two kinds of affixes:

prefixes are added to the front of words, e.g., able → enable, happy → unhappy

suffixes are added to the end of words, e.g., wide → width, wise → wisdom, offend → offensive.

- Prefixes
  positive to negative: happy-unhappy; satisfied-dissatisfied; eligible-ineligible
  verbs: large-enlarge, tell-foretell, charge-overcharge

- Suffixes
verb-noun:	approve-approval, suspect-suspicion, speak-speech
noun-adjective:	hope-hopeful, noise-noisy
verb-adjective:	widen-wide, repeat-repetitive
adjective-noun:	long-length, mad-madness, wise-wisdom
verb-adjective:	falsify-false

- Traps to beware of:
  Spelling
  Very often the base word changes when the affix is added, as in *wide – width*, *satisfy – satisfactory*

  -ible or -able
  If in doubt, use -able. The rule of thumb is that if the root is a recognisable noun or verb, the adjective will end in -able: *rely – reliable*, *value – valuable* (*capable* and *probable* are exceptions).

  The double change
  You may have to make more than one change to the base word, e.g. the meaning of the sentence requires not *satisfactory* but *unsatisfactory*, which you have to form from the base word SATISFY.

Note: in the exam, correct spelling is required.

53 Word building 1

Read the text below and use the word given in capitals at the end of each line to form a word that fits in the space in the same line. There is an example at the beginning (0).

HOW MUCH ARE YOU WORTH?

An important factor to take into **(0)** _____ in trying to answer this   **CONSIDER**

question is how socially useful a person's work is, **(1)** _____ of the   **REGARD**

talents he or she may bring to it. It is **(2)** _____ accepted that   **GENERAL**

looking after the sick or taking **(3)** _____ for the education of the   **RESPONSIBLE**

young is a more **(4)** _____ occupation than, say, selling second-hand   **VALUE**

cars. Yet used-car **(5)** _____ undoubtedly earn more than the   **SELL**

nurses or teachers. But what about job **(6)** _____ ? People who   **SATISFY**

enjoy their jobs, the **(7)** _____ goes, get their reward in the form of   **ARGUE**

a 'psychic wage', and that it is the people with the **(8)** _____ jobs who   **REPEAT**

need more money. Whatever the **(9)** _____ , jobs which are traditionally   **TRUE**

thought of as 'vocations' continue to be **(10)** _____ badly paid, while   **RELATE**

other jobs, such as those in the world of entertainment, carry **(11)** _____   **FINANCE**

rewards out of all proportion to their social worth.

Write your answers here:

0	*consideration*	**6**	_____
1	_____	**7**	_____
2	_____	**8**	_____
3	_____	**9**	_____
4	_____	**10**	_____
5	_____	**11**	_____

54 Word building 2

Read the text below and use the word given in capitals at the end of each line to form a word that fits in the space in the same line. There is an example at the beginning (0).

THE ELEPHANT MAN

John Merrick was one of the most **(0)** _____ human beings who   ORDINARY

ever lived. He suffered from a rare bone disease which **(1)** _____ him   FORM

grotesquely: his right leg was twice normal size and his head was **(2)** _____   LARGE

and misshapen. When young he had a 9-inch **(3)** _____ protruding from   GROW

his mouth, hence the **(4)** _____ nickname 'The Elephant Man'.   FORTUNE

He was **(5)** _____ seen by an eminent surgeon, Frederick Treeves, while   EVENT

working in a circus. Treeves secured his **(6)** _____ to the London   ADMIT

Hospital and gave him a mask to wear so as not to **(7)** _____ others.   TERROR

Treeves discovered that Merrick was a man of **(8)** _____ intelligence.   STAND

Treeves' friends began to visit Merrick, and his **(9)** _____ soon spread.   FAMOUS

Members of the Royal Family, **(10)** _____ Princess Alexandra, were   NOTE

among those who repeatedly visited him. The **(11)** _____ of his soul had   BEAUTIFUL

finally escaped the prison of his body.

Write your answers here:

0	_extraordinary_	6	_____
1	_____	7	_____
2	_____	8	_____
3	_____	9	_____
4	_____	10	_____
5	_____	11	_____

55 Word building 3

Read the text below and use the word given in capitals at the end of each line to form a word that fits in the space in the same line. There is an example at the beginning (0).

GESTURES

An ancient Chinese proverb says: 'Be **(0)** _____ of a man	**SUSPECT**
whose stomach does not move when he laughs.' The **(1)** _____	**MOVE**
we make with our bodies, often quite **(2)** _____ , give us away.	**CONSCIOUS**
For example, fidgeting is a sure sign of **(3)** _____ in young children.	**BORE**
Drumming your fingers on the table tends to indicate **(4)** _____ .	**PATIENT**
A man who keeps adjusting his tie is betraying his **(5)** _____ .	**NERVOUS**
These are obvious gestures, **(6)** _____ recognised and understood. But	**WIDE**
the **(7)** _____ of a gesture can vary in different cultures. The 'thumbs up'	**SIGNIFY**
sign indicates **(8)** _____ in some countries, but in others, it is obscene	**APPROVE**
and **(9)** _____ . Eye contact is another important way in which we	**OFFEND**
signal our **(10)** _____ : but at what point does a look become a stare?	**INTEND**
And when does staring rudely become gazing in **(11)** _____ ? The	**ADMIRE**

answer is, as usual 'It all depends'.

Write your answers here:

0	*suspicious*	6	_____
1	_____	7	_____
2	_____	8	_____
3	_____	9	_____
4	_____	10	_____
5	_____	11	_____

56 Word building 4

Read the text below and use the word given in capitals at the end of each line to form a word that fits in the space in the same line. There is an example at the beginning (0).

A YOUNG WOMAN TALKS AMBITION

Getting to the top doesn't just depend on (0) _____ : it also   ABLE

means making a total (1) _____ to your job. I work hard: evenings,   COMMIT

weekends, whatever it takes, I think that's why I'm (2) _____ .   SUCCEED

The people I work with are (3) _____ motivated. I work to weekly targets   HIGH

and I achieve them. Now, I'm looking for a major (4) _____ . I   PROMOTE

didn't think I was (5) _____ until I came into this environment.   COMPETE

I took a drop in salary when I took this job, but it has (6) _____   CERTAIN

been (7) _____ . I work hard and have a positive attitude to life.   WORTH

That's (8) _____ why I'm now earning the sort of salary   DOUBT

which was once beyond my (9) _____ dreams!   WILD

As to (10) _____ ambitions, well, I would like one day to have my   FULFIL

own company. But that's (11) _____ to happen for a long time,   LIKELY

if at all.

Write your answers here:

0	_ability_	6	_____
1	_____	7	_____
2	_____	8	_____
3	_____	9	_____
4	_____	10	_____
5	_____	11	_____

57 Word building 5

Read the text below and use the word given in capitals at the end of each line to form a word that fits in the space in the same line. There is an example at the beginning (0).

SHARING

Judging from the 'Flats to Let' column, there is an **(0)** _____ **END**

search going on for flatmates which is **(1)** _____ to the **COMPARE**

search for suitable **(2)** _____ partners. **MARRY**

Indeed, the fact that the **(3)** _____ often specify the type and the **ADVERTISE**

personality of the potential flatmate suggests that **(4)** _____ **COMPATIBLE**

is as **(5)** _____ in flat-sharing as it is in the person you marry. **DISPENSE**

People usually ask for or offer **(6)** _____ , but these probably provide **REFER**

only a few **(7)** _____ facts. The things you really want to know **SIGNIFY**

about a person are **(8)** _____ revealed, things like whether they **RARE**

make a noise when they eat, and other **(9)** _____ habits. **BEAR**

Let's face it, if you are going to share your **(10)** _____ with a complete **LIVE**

stranger for any **(11)** _____ of time, you need to find out at the outset **LONG**

whether their company will turn out to be a delight or a nightmare!

Write your answers here:

0	_endless_	6	_____
1	_____	7	_____
2	_____	8	_____
3	_____	9	_____
4	_____	10	_____
5	_____	11	_____

58 Word building 6

SECTION 9

Read the text below and use the word given in capitals at the end of each line to form a word that fits in the space in the same line. There is an example at the beginning (0).

FORTUNE TELLING

We live in a (0) _____ age in which everything we do is based   SCIENCE

on rational (1) _____ and careful investigation of the facts.   DECIDE

In other words, we try to act (2) _____ and as a result of using our   SENSE

brains. But, if this is so, how can we explain the (3) _____ of   POPULAR

of horoscopes and similar ways of (4) _____ the future? I once   TELL

learned to read palms, and then tried out my newfound (5) _____   KNOW

on several friends and (6) _____ . They were amazed at the   ACQUAINT

(7) _____ of my reading of their characters and even more by   ACCURATE

my (8) _____ about their future lives, but of course there was   PREDICT

nothing (9) _____ about my palmistry: it was just intelligent guesswork MYSTERY

on my part. After all, I knew my 'victims' and could (10) _____ assess   EASY

the (11) _____ that they would travel abroad or marry or change jobs in LIKELY

the near future.

Write your answers here:

0	_scientific_	6	_____
1	_____	7	_____
2	_____	8	_____
3	_____	9	_____
4	_____	10	_____
5	_____	11	_____

122 Section 9: Use of English Part 5 Word building

Grammatical terms

Traditionally, the language is divided into nouns, pronouns, verbs, adjectives, adverbs, prepositions and conjunctions. Knowing the grammatical terms is not the same thing as knowing the language, just as knowing *about* the language is not the same thing as being able to use the language. Still, it helps sometimes to know these grammatical terms if you want to talk about the language, for example, to give or listen to an explanation of a structure.

The terms tested here are ones that are widely used by teachers and students all over the world, but you may come across others. For example, what most call the <u>past perfect</u> (*I had done*) is called the <u>pluperfect</u> by some others.

Other terms have been introduced which, though useful, are not widely known. For example, <u>determiners</u> (*a*, *the*, *this*, *that*, etc.), <u>distributives</u> (*each*, *every*, *all*, etc.), <u>quantifiers</u> (*much*, *many*, etc.). We have not tested these, but you may come across them in more modern grammars.

59 Grammatical terms and verb tenses

A Which grammatical term can you use to describe the words or phrases in bold type in the sentences below? Choose from the following. There is an example at the beginning (0).

adjective	_____	adverb of manner	_____
adverb of frequency	_____	comparative	_____
conjunction	_____	definite article	_____
idiom	_____	indefinite article	_____
interrogative pronoun	_____	noun	_0_
personal pronoun	_____	possessive pronoun	_____
preposition	_____	question tag	_____
reflexive pronoun	_____	time expression	_____

0 Put the **book** on the table, please.

1 A BMW is **more expensive** than a Fiat.

2 My uncle is **an** accountant.

3 Where were you **the night before last?**

4 She was wearing a **beautiful** dress.

5 He met his wife **at** a party.

6 We **usually** play tennis at weekends.

7 **Whose** are these keys?

8 Did your son really paint this **himself?**

9 Is this **the** DVD you borrowed from me?

10 She couldn't go to the party **because** she was feeling ill.

11 'Whose pen is this?' 'It's **mine**.'

12 He always drives very **carefully**.

13 'I love **you**,' he whispered.

14 My brother **got the sack** last week.

15 He's French, **isn't he?**

B In the following groups of words, four have something in common, grammatically speaking. The fifth is the 'odd one out'. For each group, find the odd one out and explain why it does not belong with the others. There is an example at the beginning (0).

0   A think   B took   C spoke   D left   E went

The answer is A. All the others are verbs in the past tense.

1   A good   B fat   C difficult   D beautiful   E very

2   A furniture B police   C people   D cattle   E dice

3   A during   B while   C when   D as   E since

4   A lodgings B clothes   C premises   D news   E minutes

5   A my   B hers   C our   D their   E its

6   A bread   B advice   C information D homework E company

7   A away   B by   C through   D above   E with

8   A sheep   B series   C horse   D deer   E species

9   A nearly   B scarcely C hardly   D lively   E generally

10 A billiards B scissors   C athletics   D measles   E mathematics

60 Verbs

Which verb forms or tenses are shown below? Choose from the following. There is an example at the beginning (0).

auxiliary verb	_____	conditional	_____
future	_____	future continuous	_____
future perfect	_____	gerund	_____
imperative	_____	modal verb	_____
passive	_____	past continuous	_____
past perfect	_____	past perfect continuous	_____
past simple	_0_	phrasal verb	_____
present continuous	_____	present participle	_____
present perfect	_____	present simple	_____

present continuous with future meaning _____

present perfect continuous _____

present simple with future meaning _____

---

0 She **wrote** her first novel at the age of nineteen.

---

1 Fifty people **were killed** in the explosion.

---

2 He **has been teaching** English as a Foreign Language for ten years.

---

3 Our team has had a **winning** streak lately.

---

4 Do you like **singing?**

---

5 **If it stops** raining soon **we'll go** to the beach.

---

6   At 8 o'clock last night I **was walking** home through the park.

7   Janet **is having** a party on Saturday.

8   By this time next year they **will have been married** for twenty-five years.

9   The coach **leaves** Swansea at 8.20 and **arrives** at Heathrow at 11.45.

10   **I'll meet** you on Friday outside the station.

11   **Have** you ever met David Brown?

12   She was very nervous as she **hadn't flown** before.

13   Just think. This time next week **we'll be lying** on a beach in Bali.

14   I **haven't played** rugby since I left school.

15   We **had been waiting** for nearly forty minutes when the train finally arrived.

16   Jeremy **likes** classical music.

17   It's nearly seven thirty. **Wake up** everyone!

18   Peter **is walking** to school.

19   I've decided to **take up** French.

20   You really **ought** to give up bungee jumping – it's so dangerous.

Answers

Test 1

1. had been stolen
2. phoned
3. leaving
4. returned
5. found
6. had been brought back
7. was
8. opened
9. found
10. apologizing
11. wrote/had written
12. did not have/didn't have
13. had gone
14. hoped
15. did not/didn't/wouldn't   mind
16. had taken
17. (had) enclosed
18. were
19. had been trying
20. had
21. had expected
22. were
23. decided
24. got
25. was awaiting/awaited
26. had been burgled
27. had been stolen
28. knew
29. lying
30. recognized
31. saying
32. enjoyed

Test 2

1D 2A 3C 4B 5A 6A 7C 8C 9A 10A
11C 12B 13D 14D 15B

Test 3

A
1. broken off
2. broke in
3. break up
4. broke away

B
1. brought on
2. bring up
3. bring out
4. brings back

C
1. call for
2. call off
3. call on
4. called ... after

D
1. came across
2. come round
3. come into
4. come out

E
1. call for
2. bring up
3. call on
4. come out
5. break down
6. come across
7. bring on
8. break in
9. call off
10. come round
11. bring back
12. come into

Test 4

A
1. fell over
2. fallen out
3. fall for
4. fell through

B
1. get back
2. get to/get at
3. get through
4. getting ... down

C
1. went through
2. go by
3. gone off
4. go with

D
1. keep off
2. keep up
3. keep away
4. keeping ... back

E
1. get through
2. go with
3. keep up (with)
4. get to/get at
5. fall for
6. get back
7. keep back
8. keep off
9. go off
10. get someone down
11. fall out (with)
12. go by

Test 5

A
1. Look out
2. look forward
3. look back
4. look ... up
5. look into

B
1. put out
2. put in
3. put by
4. put off
5. put down

C
1. takes after
2. taking on
3. took to
4. taken in
5. take over

D 1 look into
   2 take to
   3 put by
   4 look up
   5 put out
   6 take over
   7 put down
   8 look after
   9 take after
   10 look back

   10 at the moment
   11 in private
   12 by heart
   13 on purpose
   14 out of order
   15 at last
   16 at first

Test 6
1 pick up (picked up, picking up)
2 put out (putting you out, put out)
3 make out (make out, make out)
4 send off (sent him off, sent off)
5 go into (go into, went into)
6 back up (back up, back me up)
7 catch on (catch on, catch on)
8 turn down (turned down, Turn it down)
9 do up (do up, do up)
10 give away (gave away, give you away)
11 set out (set out, set out)
12 blow up (blow up, blew up)
13 call up (called up, call me up)
14 give up (give up, give up)
15 hold up (held up, held up)

Test 7
2f 3i 4h 5j 6a 7d 8g 9b 10e

Test 8
A At: night, once, the moment, first, last, work
   By: sight, order, air, all means, heart, mistake, night
   For: a change, sale, instance, hire, the moment
   In: a hurry, hospital, particular, private, trouble, work, order, sight, luck
   On: business, a diet, holiday, order, fire, purpose, sight
   Out of: date, sight, hospital, the ordinary, trouble, breath, work, order, luck
B 1 by all means
   2 on business
   3 on a diet
   4 by sight
   5 in hospital
   6 out of breath
   7 for sale
   8 at work/in a hurry
   9 for a change

Test 9
1 ill with
2 terrified of
3 absent from
4 proud of
5 short of
6 famous for
7 good at
8 keen on
9 friendly with
10 satisfied with
11 responsible for
12 grateful to
13 eligible for
14 jealous of
15 similar ... to
16 rich in
17 absorbed in
18 cruel to
19 serious about

Test 10
1 translated into
2 charged with
3 succeeded in
4 believe in
5 remind ... of
6 compliment ... on
7 lost at
8 arrived in
9 protect ... from
10 insure ... against
11 share ... among
12 smelt/smelled of
13 suffers from
14 feel sorry for
15 think ... about
16 apologize for
17 care for
18 prefer ... to
19 rely on

Test 11
1 make eyes at
2 have faith in
3 find fault with
4 make friends with
5 make fun of
6 take issue with
7 take offence at
8 take pleasure in
9 take pride in
10 take exception to

11 pay attention to
12 take advantage of
13 catch sight of
14 keep track of
15 make provision for
16 take pride in
17 keep track of
18 pay attention to
19 make friends with
20 find fault with
21 take advantage of

Test 12
1 in agreement with
2 in answer to
3 on behalf of
4 in common with
5 in exchange for
6 in favour of
7 on good terms with
8 in love with
9 by means of
10 at odds with
11 out of pity for
12 in/with reference to
13 with the compliments of
14 at the expense of
15 under the influence of
16 for the sake of
17 With/In reference to
18 on good terms with
19 In answer to
20 under the influence of
21 in common with
22 for the sake of

Test 13
1 In which – A
2 By which – B
3 To which – B
4 On which – C
5 From which – C
6 With which – C
7 In which – A
8 With which – B
9 On whose – A
10 From which – A
11 For which – A
12 In which – A
13 In which – C
14 On whose – A

NB It is possible to replace *which* with *what*, especially in numbers 2, 11 and 12.

Test 14

1	of	17	out	33	off
2	by	18	of	34	of
3	in	19	at	35	from
4	about	20	in	36	in
5	of	21	in/during	37	out of
6	of	22	of	38	In
7	up	23	on	39	of
8	in	24	at	40	to
9	of	25	under	41	for
10	of	26	of	42	of
11	on	27	from	43	against
12	by	28	in	44	out of
13	in	29	in	45	by
14	At	30	of	46	in/inside
15	of	31	in/inside	47	of
16	in	32	to	48	in

Test 15
A 1 a bunch of sweet-smelling yellow roses
2 has lovely soft grey fur
3 a tall middle-aged German businessman
4 brand new, three-bedroomed, semi-detached house
5 fast red Italian sports cars
6 a superb oval oak coffee table
7 this magnificent old Japanese vase
8 tasty, hot Indian meals
9 a shabby old cream linen jacket
10 huge black triangular marble statue

B 1 The children sometimes go riding on Saturdays.
2 I was only pretending! I wouldn't really have chopped your fingers off!
3 Carol's daughter plays the violin beautifully.
4 My brother nearly always finishes work early on Fridays.
5 I don't often go to the theatre. My sister, on the other hand, goes regularly.

6 I still don't understand why Joanna didn't want to come to my party.

7 George hasn't done much work so he'll probably fail the exam.

8 I completely disagree with you!/I disagree with you completely! Watching football live is definitely better than watching it on TV.

9 She's just gone home.

10 Is my omelette ready yet? I'm still waiting for the hen to lay the eggs.

Test 16

A 1k 2g 3n 4j 5d 6a 7m 8f 9o 10i 11l 12h 13b 14e 15c

B 1 would/'d give you; would/'d drink

2 will you pay

3 would not/wouldn't have happened

4 won't come

5 it had rained

6 'll/will lose

7 would not/wouldn't have taken

8 practised

9 had not/hadn't driven/had not/hadn't been driving

Test 17

1 It is bad manners to roll (=roll about) in your soup.

2 The farmer was injured with the gun the bull had.

3 The dog is fond of eating children.

4 They would prefer actors and actresses who had taken drugs.

5 The man has to wash two waitresses as well as the dishes.

6 The Queen, not the ship, slid gently into the river. It used to be normal to refer to ships as 'she'.

7 Both the other motorist and a policeman smelled of drink.

8 The adult rather than the bath has a strong bottom.

Test 18

A 1k 2a 3g 4p 5l 6m 7j 8c 9h 10f 11b 12d 13o 14e 15n

B 1 as long as/provided that

2 as soon as

3 in case

4 until

5 even though/although

6 once/as soon as

7 until/unless/even if

8 because

9 If

10 even if

Test 19

1 Do you know if Mariarosa works here?

2 Excuse me. Could you tell me the way to the station, please?

3 There are not any tickets for Saturday's performance of *Aida* left.

4 How often do you borrow books from the library?

5 Did you remember to post that letter I gave you?

6 Which of you forgot to switch off the light/switch the light off before you went to bed last night?

7 If I promise not to step on your toes, will you dance with me?/Will you dance with me if I promise not to step on your toes?

8 Are either of you interested in playing a game of tennis this weekend?

9 Do you sometimes wonder what life is all about?

10 Is there any chance of having the day off tomorrow?

11 Have you ever been to Brazil or any other South American country?

12 What time does the bus leave and can you get a coffee on it?

Test 20

1 How often does she see her sister?

2 Where does Karen's husband work?

3 How much does Paul weigh?
4 How often does the team play football?
5 How long has David lived in Australia?
6 How long did the group have to wait to get through customs?
7 What time did the family finally get home last night?
8 What colour hair does Jill have?
9 How many pairs of shoes did Sam buy in the sales.
10 Whose brother is a famous soccer player?
11 How did he pay for the goods?
12 How far is San Diego from LA?
13 Where did she meet her boyfriend?
14 What does he have for breakfast?
15 Why did they arrest him?
16 Which language did your mother speak as a child?
17 Who did this pen once belong to?
18 Who has a white sports car?

Test 21
1j 2n 3l 4h 5m 6a 7c 8g 9k 10b 11f

Test 22
1 The, an, the, –
2 a, the, a
3 The, the, the, –
4 –, –, the
5 a, the, the/an, –, the
6 –, a, –, the
7 a, –, the, the
8 –, –
9 an, –, a, the
10 –, the, The, the, –, the

Test 23
1 to hurt
2 to play
3 thinking
4 to leave
5 saving
6 wanting
7 to like
8 giving
9 meeting
10 to stay
11 talking
12 getting
13 to teach
14 to win
15 taking
16 being
17 to walk
18 to find
19 to see
20 living

Test 24
A 1 Anybody = Nobody
2 few = a little/some
3 Both = All
4 being = be
5 less = fewer
6 All = Both
7 none = neither
8 many = much
9 few = a few
10 I = me
11 be = being
12 neither = none
13 much = many
14 any = no
15 Nobody = Anybody
B 16 your own
17 who's
18 yours
19 whose
20 box of matches
21 it's

Test 25
2a 3j 4h 5d 6e 7i 8f 9c 10b

Test 26
1 some, any
2 Someone/body, anywhere
3 Anything, some, any
4 some, something
5 any, something, any
6 some, Someone/body, any
7 somewhere, Anywhere, something
8 anywhere, some
9 some, any
10 any, some
11 any, some

Test 27
1 one
2 anything
3 never
4 every
5 used
6 for
7 describing
8 else
9 hired
10 made
11 last
12 which
13 were
14 then
15 each
16 must
17 its
18 throwing
19 had
20 as

Test 28

A Make: the bed, a complaint, a confession, fun of someone, a fuss, an impression, a journey, a mistake, a noise, a phone call, a profit/loss, a speech

Do: business, damage, the garden, harm, one's best, research, the shopping, someone a favour

Have: a bank account, a barbecue, a bath/shower, a celebration, a driving lesson

B
1 had, do
2 make
3 making, do
4 makes, do
5 have, make
6 do, have
7 had, making
8 do
9 do
10 make, make
11 make
12 make
13 had, made
14 making, do
15 having, making
16 have, doing
17 make
18 have
19 made

Test 29

1B	4C	7A	10C	13C
2D	5C	8A	11B	14A
3A	6D	9B	12D	15D

Test 30

1D	4D	7B	10C	13A
2B	5D	8C	11D	14B
3A	6D	9A	12C	15C

Test 31

1C	4B	7D	10B	13D
2B	5D	8B	11C	14A
3C	6A	9A	12C	15B

Test 32

1B	4C	7C	10B	13C
2B	5B	8D	11A	14C
3A	6D	9A	12D	15B

Test 33

1A	4D	7C	10B	13A
2C	5B	8D	11D	14B
3A	6B	9A	12C	15C

Test 34

1D	5C	9A	13B	17A
2D	6A	10C	14D	18A
3B	7B	11D	15C	19B
4C	8D	12B	16C	20D

Test 35

1	from	16	had
2	decided/wanted	17	into/in
3	later/afterwards	18	no
4	with/about	19	would
5	into/through	20	time
6	its/his	21	less
7	well	22	into
8	rather	23	how
9	took	24	upset
10	belonging	25	such
11	but	26	make
12	on	27	his
13	after	28	on
14	sure/certain	29	some/a
15	being	30	has

Test 36

1	all	17	makes
2	tell/give	18	it
3	who	19	long
4	any/every	20	which
5	as	21	else
6	his	22	that
7	to	23	first
8	spends	24	anything
9	gets/gathers/takes/acquires		
10	order	25	time
11	out	26	have
12	In	27	Unlike
13	enough	28	can
14	himself/well	29	come
15	watch/see/attend	30	all
16	for/and		

Test 37

1 mad/wild/crazy
2 before
3 up/out
4 into
5 remains

6 on
7 their
8 waited
9 high/far/up
10 filled
11 one
12 that/which
13 with/among
14 more
15 together
16 on/near/at
17 until
18 top/peak
19 Once/When/After
20 ate/consumed
21 made/baked
22 in
23 other
24 their
25 way
26 at
27 had
28 below/beneath (NOT under)
29 during/throughout
30 be

Test 38
1 for
2 most
3 having
4 into
5 looking/staring
6 later
7 made
8 trouble/bother/disturb/interrupt
9 like
10 still/do
11 do
12 for
13 if
14 could/would
15 such
16 course
17 how
18 back
19 After
20 made
21 of
22 done
23 themselves

24 What
25 at
26 did
27 bill
28 for
29 why
30 covers/includes

Test 39
1 One
2 was
3 attended
4 got/found/took
5 on
6 was
7 from
8 lessons/classes/courses
9 when
10 first
11 After
12 among
13 came
14 won/gained/got
15 it
16 who
17 so
18 abroad/overseas
19 appeared/featured
20 such
21 continued
22 having
23 of
24 on
25 It
26 including/notably/particularly/
   especially
27 from/of
28 there
29 every/each
30 in

Test 40
1 whole
2 soaked
3 as
4 waiting/hoping/trying/attempting
5 So
6 come/been
7 without
8 would

9 pulled/drew/drove
10 took
11 no
12 with
13 there
14 As/Since
15 in/into/inside
16 made
17 long
18 had
19 pick
20 By
21 stopped
22 out
23 feel/get
24 of
25 must
26 look
27 with/in
28 since

Test 41
1 didn't expect
2 is famous for its
3 are different from
4 this pen belong to
5 did she refuse to give
6 did you pay for
7 I need to
8 took me twenty minutes to
9 are not allowed to smoke
10 was so stale

Test 42
1 more sleep than
2 was so horrifying
3 I have to
4 left without saying
5 apologized for being
6 had more money, I could
7 would prefer not to
8 my uncle's first trip
9 looking forward to seeing
10 spent all morning working

Test 43
1 had never seen
2 get married/are getting married
3 work(s) harder than
4 was awarded
5 work as hard as

6 was such a boring party
7 you be able to do
8 has been sent
9 died at the age of
10 he could/might/borrow

Test 44
1 is the last time
2 should not/shouldn't have stolen
3 the first time I have
4 I would/I'd have bought
5 since detectives started
6 apologized for not giving
7 told me not to
8 wish I had/I'd gone
9 had (great) difficulty in starting
10 fell out

Test 45
1 was not/wasn't well enough
2 asked me to take
3 never eaten better food than
4 have not/haven't seen John
5 too quietly
6 it had not/hadn't been raining
7 wish I could
8 in order to avoid
9 had not/hadn't behaved badly
10 the first time I have

Test 46
1 all the questions right/correct
  except
2 no point in going
3 though it was raining heavily
4 there was still no sign
5 the chances of her winning/her
  chances of winning
6 take no notice of
7 would/'d rather you didn't
8 last heard from her
9 insisted on us/our staying/insisted
  that we stay
10 I hadn't seen

Test 47
1 the	7 that	13 in
2 up	8 about	14 you
3 with	9 being	15 ✔
4 was	10 want	16 it
5 ✔	11 for	
6 at	12 ✔	

Test 48
1 after	7 come	13 inside
2 ✔	8 an	14 out
3 so	9 ✔	15 ✔
4 ✔	10 as	16 have
5 when	11 after	17 for
6 that	12 ✔	

Test 49
1 she	7 that	13 ✔
2 of	8 the	14 for
3 ✔	9 ✔	15 not
4 will	10 ✔	16 very
5 it	11 then	
6 ✔	12 try	

Test 50
1 it	7 to	13 he
2 ✔	8 far	14 off
3 for	9 then	15 if
4 ✔	10 ✔	16 ✔
5 is	11 have	
6 as	12 me	

Test 51
1 they	7 ✔	13 been
2 have	8 on	14 so
3 ✔	9 to	15 but
4 she	10 away	16 ✔
5 has	11 that	
6 for	12 that	

Test 52
1 like	7 of	13 ✔
2 ones	8 to	14 for
3 in	9 the	15 about
4 more	10 ✔	16 it
5 ✔	11 me	
6 been	12 am	

Test 53
1 regardless	6 satisfaction
2 generally	7 argument
3 responsibility	8 repetitive
4 valuable	9 truth
5 salesmen/	10 relatively
saleswomen/	11 financial
salespeople	

Test 54
1 deformed	7 terrorise/
2 enlarged	terrify
3 growth	8 outstanding
4 unfortunate	9 fame
5 eventually	10 notably
6 admittance	11 beauty

Test 55
1 movements	7 significance
2 unconsciously	8 approval
3 boredom	9 offensive
4 impatience	10 intention
5 nervousness	11 admiration
6 widely	

Test 56
1 commitment	7 worthwhile
2 successful	8 undoubtedly
3 highly	9 wildest
4 promotion	10 fulfilling
5 competitive	11 unlikely
6 certainly	

Test 57
1 comparable	7 significant
2 marriage	8 rarely
3 advertisements	9 unbearable
4 compatibility	10 life
5 indispensable	11 length
6 references	

Test 58
1 decisions	7 accuracy
2 sensibly	8 predictions
3 popularity	9 mysterious
4 telling	10 easily
5 knowledge	11 likelihood
6 acquaintances	

Test 59

A adjective – 4
  adverb of frequency – 6
  conjunction– 10
  idiom – 14
  interrogative pronoun – 7
  personal pronoun – 13
  preposition – 5
  reflexive pronoun – 8
  adverb of manner – 12
  comparative – 1
  definite article – 9
  indefinite article – 2
  possessive pronoun – 11
  question tag – 15
  time expression – 3

B 1 very – it's not an adjective
  2 furniture – it takes a singular verb
  3 when – it's an interrogative pronoun
  4 news – takes a singular verb
  5 hers – it's a possessive pronoun
  6 company – it's countable (has a plural form)
  7 away – it's an adverb, not a preposition
  8 horse – it's not plural
  9 lively – it's an adjective
 10 scissors – takes a plural verb

Test 60

auxiliary verb – 11
future – 10
future perfect – 8
imperative – 17
passive – 1
past perfect – 12
present continuous – 18
present perfect – 14
conditional – 5
future continuous – 13
gerund – 3
modal verb – 20
past continuous – 6
past perfect continuous – 15
phrasal verb – 19
present participle – 4
present simple – 16
present continuous with future meaning – 7
present perfect continuous – 2
present simple with future meaning – 9

Test Your way to success in English
Test Your Grammar and Skills

0582 45176 0

0582 45171 X

0582 45172 8

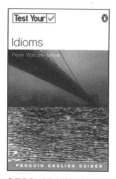

0582 45173 6

0582 45175 2

0582 45174 4

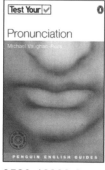

0582 46902 3

0582 46908 2

0582 46905 8